Dare To Live
Passionately

DARE TO LIVE
Passionately

by
Joe D. Batten &
Leonard C. Hudson

Resource *Publications*
An imprint of *Wipf and Stock Publishers*
199 West 8th Avenue • Eugene OR 97401

Resource *Publications*
an imprint of Wipf and Stock Publishers
199 West 8th Avenue, Suite 3
Eugene, Oregon 97401

Dare to Live Passionately
By Batten, Joe D. and Hudson, Leonard C.
Copyright © January, 1966 Batten, Joe D. and Hudson, Leonard C.
ISBN: 1-59244-232-3
Publication Date: May, 2003
Previously published by Parker Publishing Company, Inc., January, 1966.

DEDICATION

Without the faith, patience and inspiration demonstrated by each of our wives, we would not have been able to involve ourselves as deeply in the writing of this book as we have done.

It is to our wives Jean Batten and Anita Hudson that this book is gratefully and affectionately dedicated.

INTRODUCTION & ACKNOWLEDGMENTS

Leonard Hudson and I isolated ourselves in a small room in downtown Des Moines and wrote this book together. Its genesis is difficult indeed to nail down. My first book, "Tough-Minded Management," was received in a most gratifying way by the business world—both here and abroad. Its more definitive sequel, "Developing a Tough-Minded Climate . . . . for Results," was written to meet the further demand for a vigorous, vital way of business based on unflinching integrity.

"Dare to Live" was written under strong inspiration. Leonard and I are still somewhat astonished at the ease with which it was accomplished.

To my wife, Jean, goes particular gratitude. It was she who kept reiterating the need for the application of the principles of tough-minded management to the challenges and vicissitudes of daily life—particularly to family life. I asked Leonard to co-author this book because the results of our teamwork and close cooperation over the years have been a warm and fulfilling series of confrontations and victories. As a principal of our consulting firm and President of *Successful Living Institute,* he brought an impressive record of wise and significant accomplishments to the little room downtown.

To associates like Harry Willits, Jim McMahon, Edward Anson, Robert Chase, Norman Lovett, Joe McBride, Charles Richards, Dale Stouder and Ronald Pot, I say a heartfelt thanks. What can you say that's adequate about partners like Hal Batten and Jim Swab?

Jim, a charter member of our Consulting Firm, is a veritable rock whose wisdom and clear-eyed view of life has given me much.

My brother Hal's unflinching standards, candid counsel, and intellectual depth have enabled me to take many bows that should have been his. His contribution is incalculable.

To both my parents and Jean's goes the major share of gratitude for making it all possible way back when—and to Dr. Louis A. Valbracht, my Pastor, who has made the Scriptures come alive for me.

Last and most certainly not least, my secretary, Bobbie Yocum, whose steadfast dependability has meant much—and to hundreds of other friends and clients.

This book is from our hearts and we have no apology to make. There may be inadequacies—but you don't apologize when you have done your best. Whether you benefit fully is up to you. Leonard and I simply express the hope that you will read it with purpose, perseverance, pleasure and passion.

JOE BATTEN

WHAT THIS BOOK WILL DO FOR YOU

Do you react passively to life or have you learned to fling your arms wide open and welcome *confrontation—engagement—involvement* and *commitment?*

The nation—indeed the world—has an aching void . . . a hunger . . . for the big, tough-minded and passionate person (and you needn't be over five feet tall). There are more big jobs than there are big men.

Are you a member of the avant-garde? An intellectual? All right! Tackle the challenges in the book and see what happens. Purpose, poise, power can be yours. Are you timid? Shy? Tackle these challenges and discover the *real* you.

Want to feel better, live better, love better, work better? This book has the keys, the switches and the controls. You can become the generator—the transmitter—*if* you really want to.

Did you know that the Bible is the greatest psychiatric textbook ever written? Do you believe the greatest sin a person can commit is to flee through life focusing on his weaknesses and what he *can't* do? The authors do—and they show you what to *do* about it. This book says, "*Up* with people, life, love and liberty." The authors demonstrate that *downbeat* living is headed for the ashcan.

In an age that cries out, "Are we to be the last generation?", here is new and buoyant hope for a better tomorrow based upon reason, faith and love. In an age of cynicism . . . here is a fresh and confident message. In an age seemingly on the brink of megadeath . . . here is a set of steps to climb one dimension higher —to keep the Eleventh Commandment "Thou shalt love one another."

In an age suffused by a pall of nuclear fears, unleash the fresh torrents of positivism and spiritual truths which can sweep them away like papier-mâché.

Here is a book by laymen for laymen designed to help you tap into the unlimited pipeline leading from the unlimited reservoirs of God's love.

> You may have peace
> You may have power
> You may be a new person
> You may live victoriously
> You may live radiantly and passionately
> You may live abundantly
> You may plumb the depths of life's riches
> You may have unity of mind, heart and soul
> You may discover new beauty
> You may discover new creativity
> Your home may tower as a bulwark

Specific techniques and tools are provided to help you mine the mother lode of talent within you:

1. You find out how to itemize your strengths and dissolve your weaknesses.
2. You discover how to develop that elusive and vital something, the spirit that enlightens and energizes the ordinary individual so that he may accomplish extra-ordinary things.
3. You can move from segmented, sterile habits and attitudes to explosive living as a *whole* and *unified* person.
4. You can set into motion a lifetime of growth and excitement.
5. You can learn to:
    a. Understand yourself

b. Develop glowing self-confidence
c. Organize yourself—formulate your personal blueprint.
d. Dare to be a person of action—and leadership
e. Speak well
f. Understand human behavior
g. Use tension as an asset
h. Create the winning edge—self-discipline.
i. Take the herculean leap from blandness and passivity to a life of zest and passionate enthusiasm.
j. Build on your strengths and make your values work for you.
k. Learn the true meaning of complete involvement and commitment to yourself—your family—your country —your life.
l. Get out of yourself and live—become the *ultimate you.*
m. Root out hate, suspicion, fear and neurosis. Life on earth is too short for these.

Tap into the pipeline of universal power—develop the mental and spiritual muscles to turn the valves. Universal power, universal love, universal truth—it may all be grasped—if you will construct your personal beacon and let it shine forth.

In an age of over-control and seeming oppression—the truth can set you *free* to truly *live* in harmony with the laws of God and man.

Are you the "pallid leading the passive," "the bland leading the bland," or are you the "*pace* setter leading the passionate?" The choice is up to you.

CONTENTS

1 Get Out of Yourself—and Live Passionately . . . 19
Poise for Success · 19
Spiritual Engineering · 21
"The Go-Giver" · 22
Try Giving Yourself Away · 23
What Is Personality? · 24
Faith—Foundation for Success · 24
The Price Is High · 27
Dare to Live Passionately · 29
Blueprint for Happiness · 30

2 To Get Acquainted With Yourself 37
Know What You Are For! · 37
Passionate or Passive · 38
The Need for Purpose · 39
Developing Basic Beliefs · 40
The Quality of Your Mind · 41
"Tough-Minded" Living · 43
Real Masculinity—Real Femininity · 43
The Power of Love · 44

3 Unlock the Door to "Positive Successful Living" . . 47
A Positive Mental Attitude · 47
Stressing Positives for "Tough-Minded" Results · 49
The Elusive Essential—Self-Confidence · 50
"I Can" · 51
"It's in Your Power" · 52

The Seven-Day Experiment · 52
You Become What You Say · 53
No Time for Defeat · 55
The Power of Prayer · 56

4   To Be a Couragous "Tough-Minded" Person of Action   61

Internal Fibre—Needed to Fill a Bigger Mold · 61
Love—Powerful, Durable and Tough · 62
Hate—Weak, Rigid and Destructive · 63
Making Things Happen · 64
Knowledge into Action · 66
The Self-Starter · 66
Courage—Superficial or Deep Conviction · 67

5   The Power to Make Decisions   71

The Power to Choose · 71
Think with Power and Unity · 72
Make Your Values Work for You · 73
Mistakes Within Reason · 74

6   The Contagion of Passionate Enthusiasm   79

Enthusiasm, Zeal and Fervor · 79
Drudgery Depends on Attitude · 80
Vitality and Vigor · 82
Contagious Enthusiasm—Positive Emotion · 83
Tough-Mindedness as a Way of Life · 83
Think and Speak with Passion · 85
The Constructive Passions · 86
Passionate Commitment · 88
Criticism—Positive or Futile · 92
Passionate Enthusiasm · 92

7 Understanding Human Behavior 95

The Power of Projection—Strengths or Weaknesses · 95
Empathy—The Other Person's Moccasins · 96
Application of Human Understanding · 97
Basic Needs and Personal Goals · 98
Building on Strengths—Not Focusing on Weaknesses · 99
Listening—The Essential Talent · 99
Hate Is a Mask for Fear · 100

8 To Be Understood 103

The Benefits to Them · 103
Your Point—Pointed or Pointless · 104
How to Sell—Or Kill—With Words · 105
Think Big But Speak Simply · 106
Action Words and Concepts · 106
Communication by Osmosis · 107

9 Make Tension an Asset—The Music of Taut Strings 111

Live, Love and Laugh · 111
Tension—Motivating or Killing · 113
Fear—Foundation for Disaster · 114
Are They Really Out to Get You? · 116
The Business of Living a Long Time · 117
The Shift From Problems to Challenges · 120
Accept Yourself · 121
How to Deal With Tensions · 122
Make Tension an Asset · 122

10 The Unified Family 125

Unity and Faith · 125
Emotions That Destroy and Decay · 127
Emotions That Build and Enrich · 128

The Rocky Road · 130
The Warm and Wonderful Way · 132
Grow Old Happily · 132

11   The "Tough-Minded" Square 139

Return of the Square · 139
The "Tough-Minded" Square · 141
Is Graciousness Tough? · 146

12   The Winning Edge—Discipline of Self 151
Be a Giant, Not a Pygmy · 151
Take a Deep Breath · 153
The Trim Silhouette · 154
A Profile of Self—Believe In Yourself!!!! · 154
Attitudes Are the Key · 156
The Practical Man · 157
You Are No More Alive Than You Look · 157
Spiritual Power · 158
Don't Confuse Activity with Results · 160
Promises for Untapped Power · 161
Happiness—A State of Mind · 162

13   Build On Your Strengths 171
Know Thyself · 171
What Others Think · 173
Accept Yourself · 174
Focusing On Weaknesses—The Road to Oblivion · 174
Building a Positive Personality · 176
The Theory of Crutches · 177
Identification of Personal Challenges · 178
Don't Run From Success · 179

14 To Be—or Not to Be—Uncommon 181

"Un" Common as an Old Shoe · 181
(Un)Common Courage · 182
Wisdom and Logic · 183
Phonies Finish Last · 186
The Grand Design · 187
The Grand Design—In Practice · 190
The Tap Roots of Warmth · 193
The Busy Man Is the Happy Man · 195
The Snowy Heights of Honor · 196

15 No Man Is an Island 199

No Man Is an Island · 199

Appendix 1 · 205

Appendix 2 · 206

Appendix 3 · 213

Appendix 4 · 220

It is the paradox of life that the way to miss pleasure is to seek it first. The very first condition of lasting happiness is that a life should be full of purpose, aiming at something outside self. As a matter of experience, we find that true happiness comes in seeking other things, in the manifold activities of life, in the healthful outgoing of all human powers.

HUGH BLACK

1

Poise for Success

Let's take a look at the often over-worked, but usually misunderstood, term called "the American way of life." In the eyes of many people throughout the world, the American way has come

GET OUT OF YOURSELF-AND LIVE PASSIONATELY

to be symbolized by big cars, fine homes, elaborate churches, good schools and a hustle and a bustle to make lots of money. This has earned us the ridicule and contempt of many thoughtful people in many of the uncommitted nations of the world. Let's clarify here and now what the American way of life was designed to be, what it is to us, and what it can be for all.

The Constitution was designed to provide for the people of the budding United States a way of life which would provide for the execution and enjoyment of the way of living laid out by the Ten Commandments and the Sermon on the Mount. How could any American ask for a nobler framework or master structure for living? This was designed to be, and should be considered, an ideal for the rest of the world to look to with respect, with admiration and with a genuine and deep desire to emulate. The free enterprise system, which was made possible by the United States Constitution, is designed to provide for every individual in the United States four types of freedom: political freedom of enterprise, social freedom of enterprise, economic freedom of enterprise and spiritual freedom of enterprise. Increasingly, in the well-run, mature and tough-minded company we find that these four freedoms are being organized and applied to the internal affairs of the business. But business alone is not the answer. Every law office, every physician's waiting or operating room, every school, and every pulpit, must reflect a deep, meaningful and applied awareness of these freedoms. The American way of life means equality for all; a man is judged on the basis of his dignity, the quality of his mind, his uniqueness as a creature of God, and on his actual performance. No thought should be given to his particular religious denomination, the color of his skin, his ancestry or any other superficial criteria. The interesting and challenging thing is that we do not have to wait for the carefully planned and expensively produced programs made possible by our television networks to bring this about. Just a few dedicated and tough-minded people in various parts of these United States can re-examine the nature of the Constitution, commit it to memory, refresh themselves with all of the major statements in the New Testament, and relate both squarely to their daily living and working habits. Furthermore, they should consider that there is only one really good reason for any human being to march through life, and that is to reach out, to give, to build, to condition the minds and attitudes and values of others around them—to make their life more meaningful, bigger and richer.

Armed with these basic truths, and with the experiences, practices, principles, triumphs and frustrations of daily life, the articulate individual who believes in the American way as explained in this book is superbly qualified to speak out with conviction and passion, to make his views heard in any logical and reasonable time or place. This is one of the best possible ways to acquire the poise for success and a positive and dynamic program of follow-through to condition the minds and hearts of those we know, so they can truly enjoy the American way of living.

The American way of life *is* on trial! We're in hot water on a worldwide basis because millions of blind, unquestioning people have been taught to feel *passionate* about communism and socialism, even though these "ism's" have only a sterile, Godless type of "security" to offer. We have a truly great and noble pattern for living, but we cannot possibly experience total success as total people until we *understand* and *practice* these privileges with commitment and passion.

Spiritual Engineering

An *engineer* is defined as: "man who runs an engine; person who plans, builds or manages engines, machines, roads, bridges, canals, railroads, forts, etc. Expert in engineering: member of a group of men who do engineering work in the Army or Navy; plan, build, direct or work as an engineer; manage cleverly, guide skillfully." The definition of *spirit* is long, but it contains the following words repeated in abundance: "Influence that stirs up and rouses, liveliness, cheerfulness, enthusiasm and loyalty, meaning or intent, encourage, cheer, carry away, conjure up, moral, religious, emotional, supernatural, vital principle, etc.; disposition, temper, etc." If we carefully examine this rather fascinating and inspiring phrase, "spiritual engineering," we can clearly see that the principles spelled out in this book can be brought to bear with precision and effectiveness. By reducing the complex to the simple and saying, "We are out to build passion, enthusiasm, direction, energy, meaning, and vitality in our own lives," we build the spirit through engineering—first analyze, then plan, finally construct.

This entire book, the whole concept of successful living which we are building on, can be reduced to one general premise: Study, become knowledgeable, set targets and goals and then systematically lay the building blocks for the creation and growth of vitality, ebullience, zest, and pleasure—making sure that the particular building blocks are specific techniques for getting out of ourselves and into the minds and hearts of others to provide them with insight, courage, compassion, mental enrichment, emotional strength, toughness of mind—in short, a total lift of spirit. This is based upon a fundamental principle, "It is impossible to *get* more than you *give*."

"The Go-Giver"

It's impossible to give too much. The cynic can go right to this point and say, "Wait a minute, I earned the money that I have; I'm not about to give away everything that I own, my house, my car, and all my worldly goods." This is not what we're talking about at all. It's much easier to give this kind of thing than it is to give of self. It takes a much bigger person, a stronger, more dedicated and disciplined person to continuously give to others that which is most precious, most rare, and most valuable—himself.

Time and again when we have issued the challenge to people of various occupational backgrounds, dispositions, heights, weights, and ages, to devote every waking moment to reaching out and building other people, these people have come back months, weeks or years later and said, "I wonder why I didn't discover this myself. It's all so simple. I was looking somehow for a complex answer to happiness, some kind of a devious system or set of mystical formulae, some magical button to press so happiness would turn on inside of me. Instead I have found that all it takes is to get up each morning deciding that I will give a little bit of myself to every person that I come in contact with. This has made my life abundant and rich—physically, mentally, and financially, beyond my wildest imagination of some months ago."

Try Giving Yourself Away

We must be involved with people, and with society. We cannot sit back and isolate ourselves from the stream of humanity and pompously reflect on our success or our intrinsic worth. The very process of living is *involvement*. This requires commitment—a commitment of mind, heart, and body.

In order to provide you with a package of how to live with power and passion in an ever-changing, growing, and rapidly spinning world, we will discuss at some length how this ebullient new experience will make you begin to feel. We ask, "What kind of a man do you want to be?" "What kind of a woman do you want to be?" "What kind of a total life do you want to lead?" Let us examine the fundamental fact that you cannot break the Ten Commandments, you can only break yourselves upon them. What is a full, abundant and satisfying life? What is full success as a full person? Is it money? No, we know better than that now. Money is important, yes!! It can buy us many material things. It can open the door to a "golden stairway" of growth, giving and contributing, or it can virtually sentence us to a long, nameless corridor, at the end of which, stamped on a big, blank space, is the word "futility." Because, in the final analysis, those of us who set about to *get* are going to run smack up against this cold, blank square at the end of the corridor called "futility." Let's recognize it now and resolve that we will never be caught in the labyrinth of a meaningless, purposeless way of life. Let's take a long look at the Constitution and recognize that as free individuals with privileges which we retain only through discipline, that we have in reality four kinds of freedoms: freedom of social enterprise, freedom of economic enterprise, freedom of political enterprise and freedom of spiritual enterprise.

What Is Personality?

"We will be judged by what we have not done, by the love we have not shown."

Henry Drummond
THE GREATEST THING IN THE WORLD

Personality in the tough-minded living environment means the totality or sum total of a person. In short, personality means you as a total individual. What, then, is personality? Personality is made up of the attitudes, values, and beliefs that you possess. Your physical body is meaningless without the communications center which is called the human mind. So if we are going to improve our total personality, we must make sure that the mainspring stems from a mind full of the *right values*. If we set out to cultivate personality simply by reading and memorizing the statements of Emily Post, for example, we will know what to say in a given instance, but it will not come through with impact, warmth or sincerity. Seeking real success without a personal battery of positive values is like trying to look healthy solely through the use of cosmetics. Tough-minded living requires sincerity, sensitivity, and warmth. It must come from the heart and the only way in which one builds a strong and powerful mainstream between the heart and the mouth is through a strong and pervasive channel called the mind—the irreplaceable vital force.

Faith
—Foundation for Success

Just about every normal thinking adult has heard or in some way has been told that it is important to feel *faith*. Faith in who—faith in what? The question "Why is faith important?" should certainly be asked by discerning people bent on living successfully, abundantly, and passionately. Nothing, absolutely nothing, is as important for a total individual to succeed as *faith*. For this reason no business enterprise, no department, no home, school, church, or army can succeed unless they know what their objectives are.

Secondly, while knowing objectives is important, it is just a small part of the requirements for successful achievement, unless each of the persons involved *believe* in, or have *faith* in, the importance of the undertaking. Only people with a strong faith in themselves can create in their followers a belief or faith in what they are trying to get done. No leader of any kind can have real, deep sustaining faith in himself unless he first has a deep practicing faith in his own enlightened conception of a loving and all powerful God. So, before even your wife or husband can trust you, you must trust yourself—and before you can trust yourself through all of the temptations, trials and opportunities of life, you have got to be able to see yourself as a creature of individual, unique dignity and significance in the present human drama. Have I made my point? *Faith* is a better home, *faith* is a better job, *faith* is greater motivation, greater energy and certainly greater happiness.

How "practical" can you get? You can very well say, "I have experienced a practicing faith for years and I am certainly not the happiest person on my block," and we would tell you at the Successful Living Institute not to compare yourself with others, but rather compare yourself with what *you* would be without *faith* and how much greater you may become if you further develop, clarify and practice the kind of faith we have discussed.

At the very core of the tough-minded man is faith. Time after time in the business maelstrom, tired, dispirited, jaded executives have reviewed their accomplishments only to recognize that, while the sum total of their work has yielded material rewards and abundance, it has failed to provide deep down satisfaction. Most often the missing ingredient is the sort of abiding faith that supports a man in every facet of his life—a belief in God that transcends day-to-day material considerations. Is this theory? Is it pious posturing? No! To lead others effectively a man must first know himself, and to know himself he must have faith. He must know how to lose his self-preoccupation in a deep, personal commitment to eternal truths and values to his God. Tough-minded people must continuously communicate by both word and example that profit is essential, that it is honorable and that it is impossible to generate too much of it as long as the full requirements of management by integrity are met. But even more challenging, *he must blast the fallacy that you must compromise integrity to run a truly profitable business or home*—this is an absolute lie and an inexcusable fallacy.

The reverse is true in spades. Companies will always make more money when they develop the full arsenal of the tools of enterprise with the strongest emphasis on dynamic personal faith. Individuals will make the most money in the long pull if they have learned to harness, unleash and apply the tools of a dynamic personal faith. You know that you can tell the home that does not contain a deep, living and abiding faith. When you walk into such a home (the family circle of the family with faith) you don't necessarily find people who are constantly burning candles, or who are carrying out what I have called pious posturing. You don't find a group of misty-eyed dreamy people sitting around uttering platitudes either. In the family where a rich, deep abiding faith abounds you will almost always find a higher level of respect, a neater home and quite often a home that is enjoying a substantial level of material abundance. So the man or woman who wants to carry into the working place a full dynamic arsenal of tools for success can perhaps best fill the battery of his mind and soul with the material or substance called faith in the home.

"Have you heard," said the old sage thoughtfully, "about the man who arrived at the Pearly Gates and requested that St. Peter admit him to heaven?" "How are you qualified to enter here?" "I never drank, I never smoked, I never raised my voice, I never ran around with women, I never . . ." "Hold it," said St. Peter, "I'm not interested in what you *didn't* do—what *did* you do?"

The Price Is High

Brutal, stark facts are staring at us every place we look in our nation today. Phoniness and fakery are rampant. Many of the beliefs of our pioneering ancestors have become old hat, sacrificed on the altar of fakery and sham. These include:

1. Courage to work for what you want.
2. Candor—to call a spade a spade.
3. Courage to label fakery and phoniness for what it is.

Are these glittering, meaningless indictments—is this the kind of finger-pointing we have frowned on? NO!! Some actual examples of some of the degeneracy which seems to be swelling in this nation are:

1. The rise of juvenile delinquency as a product of our permissive methods of child rearing since World War II. Switch blade and black leather jacket types are not going away—they are increasing.

2. Movies and television programs which glorify the mentally bankrupt people who mumble and solve most problems by snarling and saying, "So help me, I'll kill ya." This is what we are purportedly trying to avoid developing in our children. Without a rape, incestuous or homosexual scene, most movies are currently considered bland and tepid, and we let the soft-minded "little" men who are getting rich on this kind of thing get away with it.

3. The constant search for an "angle" to get rich quick even if it involves "breaking it off" with others. An angle is rarely justified unless it is toward a positive end. For instance, Miles Standish had an angle when he asked John Alden to approach Priscilla on his behalf. Had he faced up to the requirements of the situation, he might have won her hand.

4. The willingness to surrender individuality for a government dole. When an able-bodied man seeks subsistence and sometimes even riches from the government without turning a tap, this is phoniness of the most blatant kind. This kind of search for security is indeed built on sand. It has even become very unpopular in many quarters to criticize the proliferating government hand-outs. The tragic fact is that many people simply don't *know* what is wrong with this limp pandering; they don't see that this reduces their future security to a foundation of gelatin.

5. The willingness to settle for mediocrity. Listen to the blaring, brassy, insipid, sickening music on the "top 40" which comes over the air waves. Researchers tell us that these musical offerings are aimed at the 12-year-old level. All it appears to require to be a star is a goatee, atrocious grammar, tone-deafness and utter contempt for melody. Are these the ingredients of a forward-surging culture whose past achievements have earned the respect and admiration of the world?

The "artist" who suffers for his art. Most often it appears that some of these contemporary artists suffer mostly from a need for soap, water, shaving lather and tooth paste. If our public comes to genuinely believe that welding together items of junk from a junkyard and labeling it something like "end of the world" constitutes art comparable to DaVinci then we'd better pull up short and sound off.

Writers who bat words about brilliantly only to criticize something, have been discussed elsewhere. Worse, perhaps, is the author who uses sex as his vehicle. From one torrid scene to another he marches through the book and, more often than not, winds it all up with some negative, pitiful or decaying end.

6. The apparent decline of manliness. For instance, stand on a corner in New York for about two hours. How many men will you see walk by who have their chests out, are well-

groomed, physically fit and who are not defensive or overly aggressive? We can see many pale, round-shouldered, mustachioed, "avant-garde" types. Or shift the scene to some medium-sized midwestern city and ask twenty men whom you meet, just what they intend to do to get ahead. Many of the answers will be predicated upon getting something for nothing. Or sit in a fashionable Los Angeles restaurant and listen to what some of the business people want their jobs to do *for them*.

Enough of this! A complete book should be written on the subject, but our concern here is what can the *tough-minded* person *do* about it.

Dare to Live Passionately

What creates and then extinguishes the vital spark of masculinity, feminity, or self-respect—call it what you will? This is a real, pressing, and vital matter confronting every man or woman as they move beyond the years of young adulthood.

Theodore Roosevelt, that bully old dynamo, was visited by Mike Murphy, athletic trainer at Yale. Murphy later said, "Give me sixty men, every one a champion, and let that man at Oyster Bay (Roosevelt) have sixty other men, and every one of 'em a dub, and his team could lick mine every time. That man would tell a miler that he could reel off a mile in four minutes and not only would the miler *think* he could run it in four minutes, but, by God, he'd go and do it!"

Commitment and dedication are the stuff of the really worthwhile life. Do you remember what you wanted most to do or be when you were a child? Think hard now—what happened to that dream? Did you settle for something less? Something solid and respectable? Something passive and safe? Has the spark become a blaze or has it been snuffed out? Are you living among the ashes of your past dreams or do you dare to live passionately and powerfully in the roaring flames of desire—disciplined desire—constructive, positive, piercing, pure and creative desire to make these dreams come true. Only you can answer this. The Creator meant every one of his creations to live passionately and to experience the full fruit of their manhood or womanhood. If you have a bit of a doubt about this, then read this book thoughtfully and hungrily.

Steps for Accomplishment

1. Study thoroughly in the Appendix the Ten Commandments and the Beatitudes. Determine what each statement means for you in living your life to achieve ultimate happiness.

2. Study thoroughly the Constitution (also in the Appendix) and list all of your assets that you have due to the Constitution of the United States of America.

3. Study the relationship of profit and the free enterprise system to each of the aforementioned documents. Present to yourself in the mirror the impact of profit motive on society and the free enterprise system. When you can do it competently, communicate it whenever you possibly can.

4. Apply love to everyday life. Recognize that it is impossible "to get more than you give." Be a "go-giver."

5. As you build your reservoir of resource information, begin developing your basic beliefs and establish:

>Personal philosophies,
>Principles,
>Practices, and a
>Personal faith.

6. Live and speak your practices and faith with passion!

Blueprint for Happiness

Here is a list of some of the principal qualities for the passionate tough-minded person who is not going to be satisfied to live anything less than a whole and successful life.

No. 1—No matter how you may dream, no matter how you may plan, no matter how you may wish and yearn, no matter what your heredity may be, no matter what your circumstances, you have got to be able to turn the key in the ignition with self-discipline. Self-discipline has all too often been confused with purely penalogical actions. Discipline is defined by the dictionary as "training which builds, molds and strengthens." Recognize that vigorous, outgoing ebullience as a way of life can only be possible and lasting as a product of self-discipline.

No. 2—You must recognize that developing and maintaining maximum physical fitness is an important requirement for both mental health and total financial success. Convince yourself that this kind of fitness is not self-indulgence—when you don't feel well you don't look well, you don't sound well and you don't do well. Your family suffers; you suffer. Your employees suffer; your subordinates, your superiors—everybody around you in some degree suffers when you do not feel in topnotch physical condition. So recognize how practical it is to know when to quit eating, to drink in moderation, and to learn the thrill of exercising, so that you can approach your work, the transfer of your philosophy and principles into practice, in a very fit and optimum way. To try for total success without first or concurrently making sure that you "just plain feel good" is futile. You'll accomplish much, but not nearly as much as if you take the time and effort to discipline your body so that it provides the best possible temple for your mind.

No. 3—Enjoy life and *let people know it*. The dour, scowling and formidable executive in a business accomplishes little by this behavior except ulcers for his staff and himself. The screeching, carping, harpy type of wife who doesn't enjoy life and apparently doesn't want anybody else to, is sentencing herself to mediocrity, to a grave and meaningless nothingness as the years unroll for her. But the man who has dedicated himself to the proposition that he is going to let his wife constantly know how much he enjoys life and what is good about life; the woman in kind who shows that she is going to show the man in her life that she is a joyful person (that these are essential elements of grace) have filled another essential requirement for abundant and healthful living.

No. 4—It is important to develop a broad and varied spectrum of interests and activities. There are people who feel that pouring all of their energy into one particular interest or hobby is the path to real happiness. This can be the path to a certain kind of satisfaction, but not the path to real total happiness. Extensive psychiatric, psychological and medical research has shown that the person with a broad and varied spectrum of interests and the habits which develop a broader and tougher quality of mind, will stand him in real stead as he matures beyond certain capacities and interests which he might have developed in childhood or early in adulthood. The more broadly you have prepared to expand as a total person, the more zest you get from the varied, shifting and ever-changing challenges of life.

No. 5—You must either develop or move toward a personal faith. You must visualize religion as a personal thing, a way of living, and be tolerant of others. Without faith, life becomes a meaningless scramble, a meaningless series of attempts to put more into your stomach, to surfeit yourself with the physical and material comforts of life. Millions of people have found out over the years that once you reach this level of physical and material achievement, there is still a deep hunger and yearning for something more. *Don't wait until you reach this material level of achievement to discover this hunger and this need.* The person who has a faith is more effective, he impresses his employer more, he's a bigger person, he inspires and motivates the people with whom he works better and the kind of environment that he creates around him pushes him on very surely and very steadily toward job success as well as total success.

No. 6—You should never apologize for a thing before doing it; apologize only when you know you have not done your best. You will then find very little reason ever to apologize.

No. 7—Take the stand and build into your every action, your every attitude and every reaction the belief that negativism is *never* justified. You must realize that, while there are pluses and minuses in every situation, the minuses can always become pluses if you have the dedication, the discipline and the commitment to positive living and thinking.

No. 8—Always search out and ask for the "why" of any major undertaking and make sure, in order to get the cooperation of those who work with you, that you vigorously and consistently supply the "why" to them. Real motivation, real energy and commitment is pretty difficult unless they understand why they should give you this kind of commitment and cooperation.

No. 9—Base your decisions on facts and, once you have the facts, set your goals and set a timetable, do not let the little man or the little person stand in your way. Lift him up and propel him onward. Wrench him around sharply if you have to.

No. 10—Be your own man and recognize that, while humility toward God is essential and that your own skill and confidence increases in direct proportion to this surrender, this in no wise carries over into your relations with other people. If you develop a deep and sustaining self-confidence, if you learn to assimilate and practice the other values presented in this book, if you have the proper humility with God, you will almost never be accused of any type of arrogance or exploitation with your fellow man. So cast the word humility out of your vocabulary in your relations on a day-to-day basis with your fellow man because it has no place in your relationship with mortals. Cooperation, respect, love—yes, in abundance—but not humility. Our objection to humility here is that it tends to provide a comfortable crutch and a successful, **ebullient person who walks through life with his head high should** never rely on any kind of a crutch. We have no time for it, and it is not a part of this approach to tough-minded living. God never expects obsequious, fawning or timorous behavior from his children.

No. 11—Stay completely and eternally unsatisfied with your abilities as a communicator. Strive in every way that you can think of, in addition to the ways that are outlined in here, for achieving greater eloquence in communicating your philosophy, your principles, and your practices to all of those around you. Recognize that few, if any, of us have come close to our optimum abilities as communicators. Accept this as a challenge; work at it. Study books on vocabulary; set up "think" sessions at home.

One specific device is to learn one new word each day. Write it down in three different sentences in a notebook that you keep at home. Then, sit down and review these very briefly with your family each night. You learn one new word a day that you didn't know before and in seven days you've added seven good, basic, healthy terms to your power to express yourself. Perhaps even more important you let your family participate in an intellectual adventure with you—something that adds unity and effectiveness and happiness to total family living.

No. 12—Be impatient with negative statements like "You can't teach old dogs new tricks." Modern research shows that if a person is healthy in body and has a normal mind he can learn until the day he dies. So, again, get rid of this particular crutch if you've been using it as one. Whether you happen to be twenty or sixty, resolve to learn new things until the day you die and be assured you can.

No. 13—Slice right to the heart of problems. Recognize that the roundabout way, the subtle way, the oblique way, is simply a waste of your time and the time of others and this is the kind of privilege or license we cannot take with the time of others.

No. 14—Recognize that life without work is a short cut to deterioration. When we do not have something that makes our hearts beat rapidly, that makes our senses quicken, we do not force the blood out to our extremities and we begin to dry up and wither from the outside in. Many times the kind of person who dies way before his time is the kind of person who has tried to conserve his energy, who has believed in "the bland leading the bland." The bland life, the life where one seeks to avoid stress, seeks to avoid hard work, seeks to avoid the big challenges of life —can literally lead to an atrophying, a drying up of the total body.

No. 15—Recognize that a broad and varied fund of knowledge equips you not only to be a better generalist in the business of living, but makes you also a better specialist in many ways; e.g., if you are now a personnel director and you want to be a better one, then learn more about manufacturing, learn more about purchasing, learn more about buying, learn more about selling. Suppose you are a Buyer; you can learn a lot more about buying and be a much better buyer, if you get out into the plant and find out more about the strengths, weaknesses and the problems of the materials that you have been buying and that you will be expected to buy.

No. 16—Be proud of your way of life. Make sure that you understand the Constitution; make sure that you recognize that this Constitution was created as a system of law for the practicing of the Ten Commandments in our United States. Make sure you recognize the excellence of this way of life compared with other ways of life throughout the world and then *talk* about it. Let other people in your community and in your home see and hear this. Let your children see that your pulse quickens when you think about the benefits, the challenges, the opportunities in our system of free and individual enterprise.

No. 17—Be sure to distinguish clearly between wit and intelligence, or between wit, intelligence and wisdom. Intelligence is something that we are to some extent innately gifted with when we are born. Knowledge is what we feed that intelligence with.

Wisdom is the grindstone of experience; wisdom is what we achieve through using this basic intelligence and this acquired knowledge to achieve real insight into what life is all about.

No. 18—Just one example is: true happiness will always elude you until you learn to get completely out of yourself, build and give. Strive for a balanced existence, with the full knowledge that a personality can become lopsided; all work and no play not only makes Jack a dull boy, but a pretty unsuccessful one. All play and no work can certainly make him dissolute and a soft, confused playboy. So, plan your existence to include a good amount of recreation, a good amount of work and a good amount of study.

No. 19—Stay impatient with yourself if you still have the feeling that a harried expression and an ulcer are signs of success. Recognize that you're going to have to grow up and mature beyond this or you'll never succeed.

No. 20—Be satisfied with nothing less than full success as a whole person.

There are admirable potentialities in every human being. Believe in your strength and your youth. Learn to repeat endlessly to yourself: "It all depends on me."

ANDRÉ GIDE

2 Know What You Are For!

TO GET ACQUAINTED WITH YOURSELF

It is important to know what you're *for* to develop answers to a number of questions. What kind of a mind do you want? What kind of body do you want? What kind of an image do you want to project to those with whom you work and those whom you love? What kind of a total life do you want to lead? What kind of a person do you want to be? Too many of us are articulate, eloquent and highly informed about what we are against when we should be determining clearly and comprehensively and in a very meaningful way what we are *for*. In order to do this, it's very important to make a list of what you actually stand *for* and what you are *against* at the present time.

Here's an actual example that was instrumental in the development of the book, *Tough-Minded Management*, which has provided many of the principles and concepts on which we are basing living a full, successful and abundant life. One night while sitting in one of the best restaurants in Chicago I observed a group of some forty well dressed, sophisticated-appearing, successful-looking men somewhere between thirty and forty-five. As I sat and listened to these men I became fascinated. Not one of these well dressed, successful-appearing men was saying anything that reflected the knowledge of what he was *for*. They were articulate and eloquent men, but they expressed only what they were *against*. Not one man said anything *for* an acquaintance, a subordinate, or a superior, or one of his contemporaries. The potential power within that particular group was immense if every man could suddenly change 80 per cent of the things that he was *against* to the things that he was *for*. There was enough latent strength and potential ability in that forty men to absolutely change the face of the country and perhaps of the world. But here they were frittering away, dissipating, wasting the energy of their mind, heart, and soul by simply tearing themselves up with conflict and negative, indecisive, and sometimes rather poisonous discussions of what they were against, while life was doing something *to* them instead of *for* them. There appeared to be no comprehension that they must first put much *into* life before they could begin to realize something *from* it.

Passionate or Passive

Do you have the courage and conviction to think not only with your head, but sometimes with your heart? Do you recognize the need for passion? The need for *positive passion?* Do you feel a certain necessity, as well as experience a certain thrill in expressing yourself with vehemence when you know the purpose of your statement is to *build* and *help* others? Let yourself go! Time after time—speak with passion. Don't let it worry you when inhibited, timid, pale, mousey individuals look at you disapprovingly; when they purse their lips, when they pull down the corners of their mouths and say, "He or she talks too much, gets too excited, feels too much passion." Don't let this kind of person back you off into a corner. Come on with increased vehemence as long as you are sure that your motivation is absolutely concerned not with taking, not with listening to yourself, not with getting; but with giving, building and creating.

Are you passionate or passive? Look these words up. Each has a very specific meaning—one smacks of real success—the other one smacks of real futility. Do you speak with passion or do you speak with passivity? Many people have made the mistake of confusing the life of Jesus Christ with passivity. Whereas, in reality, here was a man who lived, spoke, and conditioned every action with an all-out, out-glowing of passion. His was truly a passionate mission culminating on the cross in a moment of the most excruciating passion as he prepared to meet the Almighty Father. Examine the New Testament in the light of passivity. Ask yourself if you can find any sentence, any phrase, any word, which suggests that Christ simply adapted to his environment. In the instances where he seemingly went along with the cynical attacks of others, this was simply one additional step in carrying out his total mission. But recognize that he was always pursuing a mission, a mission that would have been impossible without passion—*positive, powerful, passion.*

The Need for Purpose

All human beings must have purpose. The only thing that adds meaning in life to these minute things that we do when we get up in the morning—brush our teeth, shave, prepare breakfast, get the kids off to school or we do this, that or the other thing—is the greater purpose they are part of. We know that at this particular point in time we have a purpose, a set of minute or miniature purposes; but do we have a clear understanding of the *total* purpose of which this is just a part?

You may have already asked yourself this in your own mind and if the answer is negative, don't let it discourage you in any way because you are part of a great majority.

We've talked to successful men, top executives, and top leaders in their professions from coast to coast and abroad, and we often find that many of these men have not clearly worked out and crystallized a basic purpose which gives their lives additional meaning. You might ask, if they're already highly successful, eminent in their profession, and well known, why they should need to define their purpose. It should be clearly understood throughout this book that at no point are we asking you to compare yourself with other people in your community or in your job. This you will do indirectly, anyway. We are asking you and challenging you to compare yourself with that particular *you* that you are now, but most important—the *you* that you *can* be.

Now, as we look at these eminent men, it's always challenging and it's always rewarding when you see them clarify and develop a real deep sense of purpose; to watch, not how far they outstrip their competitors or their contemporaries or their associates, but how much more rapidly they gain a much greater awareness and a much greater amount of accomplishment in regard to their own potential. The need for purpose is to develop it so that you can better understand and better use the potential and the power that lies dormant within you.

Developing Basic Beliefs

If you have a little child who asks you "What do you believe in?", looking to you for guidance and statements he or she can begin to use for mental and emotional security; if you're aware that what you say may be the foundation for the future success or failure of your child; if you realize that you may be preparing confident, upstanding citizens, or laying the groundwork for indecisiveness, neurosis, and psychosis—how would you answer this question? You see, I think it absolutely vital that parents have the basic beliefs to give children. I used this example so that you can see the impact on others of indecisiveness and a failure to have thought these things through. What about the benefit to you? I have never yet seen a truly successful man or woman who does not have a strong, living and breathing belief in a number of things. They believe in the basic goodness of people. They believe in the essential rightness and strength and good of our Constitutional way of life. They have studied the Constitution so that they know something about it so that it can add incentive and meaning to what they do each day. They have developed a great awareness of, a need for, and appreciation of, their particular concept of the Creator, whether they be a Christian, Jew, Mohammedan or whatever. They discovered that a belief in an Almighty and a deep, personal commitment to their Almighty is absolutely essential to true success. So, let nobody mislead you, and certainly do not mislead yourself, that you are capable of lifting yourself up by the bootstraps without a set of beliefs or without a deep and practicing faith that you can achieve great success. You may achieve substantial success, but great success will only come when you can define the basic beliefs that add energy to your particular fuel tank, that add direction and meaning to your life.

The best way to recognize dignity is in the *achievement* of the person.

The Quality of Your Mind
When we take a look at the typical business or professional office we must see that the secret of success is not some mysterious manipulation of the equipment or of the forms, or some particular plan for demolishing your opposition or the competition of the businessman. When we back off, whip out the big lens and take a real look at any enterprise, what do we see? We see five basic resources: men, money, materials, time and space. We can define the management of any enterprise as the **efficient and economical use of men, money, materials, time and**

space to achieve a predetermined objective. Sounds nice as well as academic, but it means very little.

We can move a step further toward definition by saying the most important of these resources is men; that materials, money, time and space are meaningless without well-selected, well-trained and well-motivated men. This is perhaps a new way of looking at it for some of you, but it's insufficient to give us the real answer. Let's take, then, just a group of men working together. When we step up the power of this microscope or of this magnifying lens, we'll see that the body of men—the kind of clothes they wear, the chic appearance of the woman—all these things are meaningless unless we find in the mind of each one a certain set of qualities.

What is the mind? What should it be? What constitutes "quality" of mind? What constitutes the successful mind? What constitutes the confused or the shrouded mind? The grim mind? The morbid mind? What constitutes the enlightened, the zestful, freewheeling mind? The mind of the big person? The mind that is one with a powerful and meaningful soul? The answers to these questions determine the quality of your mind.

It takes no brains and no guts to determine what you're against; anybody can do this. The hard mind is much like a piece of cast iron; it's rigid, it's hard, but it's weak. If struck a certain blow it would shatter. The tough mind is like a piece of leather—you can hit it the same blow and it simply becomes dented and even that dent springs back a little bit. Because it is fibrous it is pliant, it is flexible and it is tough.

Then many people begin to congeal, to get hard and rigid, and when adversity hits—deaths in the family or financial failure, illnesses, or a number of reverses—then the hard personality falls apart because it is only hard and not tough. But the kind of personality that is tough survives and becomes stronger and stronger as adversity strikes. This is based upon the quality of mind that is thoroughly aware of basic values and beliefs. This so often is the kind of person who in his 80's or 90's is called "the sprightly oldster."

"Tough-Minded" Living

Some of the things we have already talked about are the importance of knowing what you're for, your success profile, and a feeling of purpose and direction, so that you can fuse and focus your energies. You need a set of personal beliefs that give you additional strength, vitality, and energy. All people have basic dignity and should be judged by their dignity instead of what they seem to be. All of these are parts of living the tough-minded life. In this particular chapter all we can do is to help quicken your pulse a little bit with the actual promise that you can and you will develop a tougher, more meaningful, durable, lasting quality of mind that should contribute to the enrichment of family life; that should contribute to the view that people of your community take of you; that should enable you to go to bed at night and go to sleep with a clear conscience that you've given something that day; that you've made the earth just a little bit better place; that has stirred within you a happy dissatisfaction with what you have not been able to do, rather than just simply a negative preoccupation with what others may seemingly have done to you.

Real Masculinity—Real Femininity

These are some of the basic strands of the fabric called "tough-minded living." I would wager that every woman reading this book wants to be a truly feminine individual, and each man wants to be truly masculine. Yet, in the case of a lot of people we're missing the boat very badly because somehow we've confused masculinity with being hard, hot tempered, using force, flexing muscles, and crippling, cutting sarcasm. We've confused *hardness* with *toughness*—but the toughest, most powerful quality of mind is the emotion of love. The weakest and most meaningless, watered down, poisonous, adulterated form of emotion is hate. Therefore, to be truly masculine you must understand and you must live, breathe, and apply love toward all those with whom you work and live. To be truly feminine you must understand why, and develop an ever-increasing proficiency in the application of love for all the people with whom you associate.

The Power of Love

Ever since the history of the twelve tribes of Israel, we have had not thousands, but millions and millions of people try to solve the problems of the world through hate and its many manifestations. Strange as it may seem—and it is so simple, so basic—we often overlook this very potent solution because often we're looking for a complex solution to the problems of our life. A very minute number of people have tried to solve the problems with which they are surrounded by reacting with love toward all situations.

Let me now give you some of the ways in which the apostle Paul broke down the anatomy of love. Let me list for you, ask you to thoroughly memorize and to think deeply about these particular parts or manifestations of love, as follows: Let's call it the Anatomy of Love and list the following nine components. They are: patience, kindness, generosity, humility, courtesy, unselfishness, good temper, lack of suspicion, and sincerity. I think that all of us in the deep recesses of our minds will admit when we're simply lying in the dark and communing only with ourselves, that we would like very much to be able to apply these things. Instead, we so often use words like "distasteful, odious, despise, hate, dislike." These terms simply describe what we're against. In your experiments, experiment with a smile at a stranger in a hurried or tense situation, such as in heavy traffic. If you smile, they will—if you look angry, so will they—and you will find you will feel much better for the smile.

Do you have the courage and the intelligence to meticulously examine all of the things that you are against in your life up to this point and set the goal of converting every one of those to a statement and a belief in what you are for?

Steps for Accomplishment

1. Recognize the difficulty of seeing you as you are.
2. Determine what you are for!
3. Determine your strengths—don't focus on your weaknesses. Ask what, when, where, how and why about yourself. Write down your strengths so you can keep them readily in front of you.
4. Based on your basic beliefs and values, establish in your mind your purpose for living.
5. Live your life as if you were the person you want to be—and you will be that person.
6. Remember—like begets like; good begets good; evil begets evil. In modern jargon: the output of a computer is only as good as the input. As programmers say: Garbage In—Garbage Out (gigo).

You can do what you want to do, accomplish what you want to accomplish, attain any reasonable objective you may have in mind—not all of a sudden, perhaps not in one swift and sweeping act of achievement—but you can do it gradually, day by day and play by play, if you want to do it, if you work to do it, over a sufficiently long period of time.

WILLIAM E. HOLLER

3 A Positive Mental Attitude

UNLOCK THE DOOR TO "POSITIVE SUCCESSFUL LIVING"

Let's take a look at Bert, how he lives, and a few things about him. Bert F. is forty-four; he is head of a major department in a medium-sized company. You can call it a bank, a store or a manufacturing plant. He pulls into the driveway of a house that costs somewhere between $20,000 and $35,000. Sometimes he reaches—a little convulsively—for a drink as soon as he gets home; but at other times he doesn't need one at all. He usually is glad to get home, although he often paces restlessly about the living room, later in the evening. He doesn't know exactly why. He has some vague uneasiness and often becomes restless on Sunday because of a vague mixture of both dread and anticipation about going to work on Monday. He is getting a little thick around the waist. He finds he is increasingly wearing out the heels of his shoes rather than the front of them. He wonders from time to time whether his wife and family really love him or just the standard of living he provides. He is beginning to take note of every newspaper article about men who have heart attacks in their forties and fifties. He's a little puffy-eyed; he wonders whether the women still see him as a pretty virile and attractive guy. He vaguely yearns for a chance to prove it to a few of them. He has a good steak whenever he wants it. He buys good bourbon. He has two cars. His family does not lack any material necessity; indeed, they have a number of luxuries. He often has the feeling his subordinates are after his job and finds himself becoming defensive and/or sarcastic with them. Tensions develop—though never serious—between him and his boss. He can seldom put his finger on the reason for these tensions. He has vague fears and cannot identify them. He has become quite uncertain of what success really is! ! ! ! He is hungry for something, but he doesn't know what; he is tired. He may drop dead in a few years or in a few months. He has a better bank balance than he dreamed of when he was a boy. He has a better car, better home and his children are going to better colleges. What's missing? *Real* happiness, *real* success—that's what is missing!

Well, we are talking about approximately 80 per cent of the adult people in this age group in the United States when describing the particular plight of Bert F. So what's needed? What, then, will provide a man like Bert with the keys to really positive, successful living? One of the first requirements is a positive mental attitude.

Perhaps the most important word in the whole concept of living successfully is the word "belief." Belief in yourself, belief in your country, belief in mankind, belief in God. And once you've learned to practice all day long a belief in your ability to get a thing done, few people can stand in your way. Consider the old Latin proverb: "Believe that you have, and you have it."

Stressing Positives for "Tough-Minded" Results

It's important to recognize that positive thinking is not simply a Pollyanna-ish type of phrase. Recognize that it does not simply consist of saying, "Every day in every way I am getting better and better," with the far, dreamy-eyed hope that this is going to make everything all right. It won't. It's important to make as sure as you can, to the greatest extent possible, what the facts in a situation are. Based on an analysis of those facts then, set your goal; determine what you are going to get done on a day-to-day basis, weekly or monthly basis, or in terms of your total life goals. And then resolve to get there and don't let little people get in your way.

Living positively and benefitting from the application of positive thinking involves not only a few major statements to make each day or a few major actions. Convert the whole concept of living from negative to positive. Set out to discuss with your wife, your husband or your closest friend all of the little ways in which you may be sounding negative, in which you may be conditioning your thoughts, words and actions by what you're against instead of what you're for. Maybe it's a tone of voice. Maybe you've got a rough edge there that you should *clear up* a bit. Maybe you've got a querulous whine. Maybe you've got a questioning cynicism. Maybe you focus on the weaknesses of people instead of talking about their strengths. Maybe you are constantly looking for reasons to fail instead of reasons to succeed. The only person who can convert you from a negative thinker to a satisfying, positive way of living is *you*, but it takes guts and it takes self-discipline. Do you have it?

The Elusive
Essential—Self-Confidence

The most scarce ingredient in business and daily living today is deep, sustaining self-confidence. Why is this important? Have we not been advised by the Sermon on the Mount to feel meek, to practice meekness? Yes, this kind of meekness toward our Creator is absolutely essential and vital to a successful life, but it shouldn't be confused in any way with self-confidence, because the Almighty intended that every man and every woman should walk tall with confidence in himself. Based on the premise that until you know what your strengths are (until you know what you have to give) you can't give much and nobody can be considered successful at the end of this mortal life unless they have given much. Thus, we feel that any person who can meet his Maker with a clear conscience and sit back and figuratively add up his assets and liabilities when the time comes to leave this earth, will probably depart with much less than satisfaction if he knows he hasn't given, only taken. The only way you can give is first to know what you've got to give. And this can come only from a realistic, positive analysis of your strengths, what you are for and the determination to constantly expand these, increase them, improve them, to take on challenges, to take on adversities, and to deliberately cultivate difficult and developmental situations.

If you have deep, sustaining confidence based upon a realistic evaluation of your abilities and a true humility toward God, then this is something that you can proudly say—and don't confuse real self-confidence with egotism or self-seeking vanity or posturing or preening or anything of this kind—deep, sustaining self-confidence is a wonderful, essential way of living. True humility is impossible without real self-confidence and real confidence is impossible without real humility toward God. If you check the word "meek" as used in the Sermon on the Mount, you will find the original Aramaic language defined it in much the same way as we use the word "tough."

"I Can"
Write down on a piece of paper now in large, printed capital letters, "I CAN'T." Look at it a little bit. How do you feel when you look at the words? Does it bring out any challenge? Does it bring out any warm glow? Notice, the longer you look at these words, "I can't," the more you seem to figuratively pull away from that sheet. You pull away; your mind stops whirring with the enthusiasm that you already had and suddenly your machinery seems to be kind of thrown into neutral. Your thoughts begin to congeal. A certain something leaves your manner, your enthusiasm, as you look at these words. What does it mean? Is there *ever* any merit in saying "I can't?" Until you've given a thing a real good try, until you've researched the facts and you've decided why you should do it and given it a heck of a good try, there is absolutely no merit backing away from the thing and saying "I can't."

In the book *Tough-Minded Management* I said: "Never apologize for a thing before doing it; apologize only when you know you have not done your best." Let this little phrase sink into your mind and *think* about it over and over again. I think you will see a lot of power here. Never apologize for a thing before doing it; *apologize only when you know you have not done your best*. The interesting thing here is that there will practically never be any reason for any kind of an apology. If you consistently approach a thing with the belief that you *can* and you defer it, and you do not begin to build around you a negative set of reactions by starting to apologize (by giving people a reason to doubt your ability to do so) you will almost always get it done, and an apology afterwards will never be forthcoming because you will also have done your best in the process.

Do you have the brains and the guts to do this? It is awfully easy to hide behind this very comforting and soothing crutch called "I can't." Let me suggest now that you take your pen or pencil and strike out with a bold stroke—the "t."

"It's in Your Power"
One of the deluding types of emotions that we have, the kind of thing that stands in the way of success and real living, is the feeling that you can't do much about the world around you, that it's in the hands of other people. It's very convenient to blame the government; blame the state of the world for anything that goes wrong. Or, it can be comforting and it can be deadening and can destroy your potential for success because the power for success lies in only one person and that is *YOU*. It's in your mind. The quality of mind that you have is the only thing that is going to determine the extent of your success. So cast away, pull away and then throw away every crutch: words like "I can't," words like "They're out to get me," words like "This government of ours has destroyed the opportunity for free enterprise, it has destroyed the opportunity for a man to succeed." Because, the time for opportunity is greater in this country of ours today than it has ever been in the recorded history of the country. The opportunities in the world today for people who think and work and talk like giants instead of pygmies are absolutely unlimited. There are far more big jobs than there are big men, but "It's in your power; it's up to you and nobody else."

The Seven-Day Experiment
If you want to be sick and weak and neurotic seven days from now, with a fog of greyness hanging over your mind, where you feel absolutely lousy, you can do it and here's the way. Decide that you're going to spend every waking moment thinking only of yourself; thinking of *me, me, me, I, I, I*. To heck with everybody else, I'm looking out for me. I'm going to analyze every little burp and every belch and every little rumble that I have. I'm going to make sure that everything that people say to me is carefully studied in terms of what they mean

to me. I'm going to make sure that when I leave a tip for a waitress that she knows that *I* gave it to her and that she knows that *I* did it because *I*, big me, am generous. I'm going to talk about *me* and think about *me* and go out to simply *get* for seven days. You can make the next seven days the most miserable, despicable, grey type of existence you can imagine. You say to yourself: "Well, by gosh, without really making an effort I've been doing a good bit of that my whole life." You've certainly got a lot of company.

Now, what about this challenge for the seven days? You can make the next seven days the most glorious, the most wonderful and the most stimulating and developmental that you've ever spent if you'll do this: Simply reverse the process I've just described 100 per cent and decide that every waking moment is going to be spent completely *out of yourself*. Get *out of yourself* and *give* something to every person with whom you come in contact. We're not talking about writing him a check for $50.00; we are talking about *giving* something that's *much more precious* and that is *yourself*. The money that you have to give is not nearly as valuable as the encouragement, the product of your mind, the warmth, the understanding, the love, the guidance and the uplift. Give this and give it completely in an unrestrained, all-out way to all of the people around you for seven days. Now, it's going to take guts; it's going to take more discipline and courage than you've probably ever used before. The rewards can make of you a truly successful, big and happy individual. Try this experiment. It can add a real new dimension to your life.

You Become What You Say

Decide to experiment for a day on saying "I can't" to just about everything that comes up. Look out for yourself, say "I can't," decide that people are out to get you, make of negativism for one day the creed that I mentioned a moment ago and see what happens. Talk this way. Maybe you don't think it, but just talk it for one day and see what happens.

You may internally be filled with a buoyant positivism; you may be already applying the power of the principles we've been talking about, but just try "I can't" for your own edification for one day and by the end of that day you're going to have a bad taste in your mouth. You're going to make some slight enemies that day —perhaps no real overt enemies—but you're going to watch people shy away from you, pull away from you. You're going to watch a certain chilliness develop when you walk into the supermarket or when you walk up to the water cooler or when you walk into the lunchroom or wherever it may be, because people don't like that kind of person around and *"you become what you say."* If you set out then to talk for quite a number of days in a completely negative way in spite of what else you've learned here, you can still become a very negative and thoroughly repulsive individual. But, again, let's reverse the process. Decide that even though you have some negativism in you now, that the twenty-five, the thirty-five, the forty-five years that you've spent can't be overcome and changed overnight, but you recognize that you've got some of this and you don't want it.

You do become what you say. Set out, then, to memorize every kind of positive way of expressing yourself you can think of. Base it on "I can." Base it on the belief that people are fundamentally good. Base it on the fact that love is a powerful and exacting emotion—that it's big, that it's manly or that it's womanly, as the case may be. Say these things. Use words like "excellent;" use stretching words. Eliminate words like "morbid, sickly, turbid, grey, average, status quo," etc. Start using crisp, crunchy phrases. Start saying "I can;" start saying "I want facts," "I want goals and then I'm going to move toward them and I'm not going to let the little person get in my way." If you decide that you're going to become a totally successful person then sprinkle and saturate everything that you say with success terms. Use these words; they may seem strange at first. They may be awkward as an addition to your vocabulary, but use them and then start watching expressions. Watch the people's reaction; it's going to be a pretty wonderful thing.

No Time for Defeat

Sometimes certain executives for whom we have a high regard may be seen by some of their subordinates as slightly abrasive because they say, "I've got no time for negative talk; I've got no time to listen to the person who believes it can't be done. I don't want any 'abominable no-man' in my organization. I don't want a bunch of Pollyanna, misty-eyed dreamers who say, 'Every day in every way I'm getting better and better' and let it go at that without converting it to action." "I want people around me who believe in the timeless truths; I want people around me who believe that it is absolutely essential to have goals company-wide, departmentally and for each individual. I want people around me who have the self-discipline to do things after I simply outline the end results that I want. I want people around me who know what they are for and who are impatient with people who want to talk about what they're *against*. I want men around me, in short, who are big men, even if only five feet two. I want to associate with women who are feminine. I want to associate with women who have a deep understanding of the dignity and the honor and the sheer joy of being a woman. In short, I do not want people around me who want to discuss defeat, who think in terms of defeat, who condition and saturate everything that they say and do with the imminent possibility of defeat."

This is not because of an impatience, it is because these executives recognize that when people become affected by, when they become obsessed by the fact that they may be defeated, *they are probably going to be defeated* and the only people they are hurting and damaging are themselves and their loved ones. So, this type of impatience is caused not by any negative anger toward these people but because of the disappointment that they are overlooking the potential for a much bigger, better and more wonderful life.

The Power of Prayer

It does seem ironic sometimes that we should have to point out, in view of the many articulate, capable and wonderful men that we have in the ministry, the power of prayer to a lot of people. But the bald fact is that a lot of people who need it the most don't go to church and some who go to church have listened day after day, year after year, and never discovered that prayer is not a perfunctory thing. When a person arbitrarily says to his God, "Now, then, I want You to do this for me; I want this. I want You to make so-and-so well; I want thus and so for me." He says in effect—"If I don't get this then I'm not going to believe in You"—how childish and ridiculous can we be? Anybody who has made any depth study in any thoughtful way at all of the nature of God's will does recognize that God is love and that God answers only those who approach Him through prayer in a manner calculated to give. We obviously have no way of knowing precisely what God thinks or does; this would certainly be presumptuous to comment on. I know from experience and the experience of many men with whom I've built warm and satisfying and fine relationships that there are some ways to go about praying; and first of all the thing that you don't do is to ask for something for yourself unless you are asking for something that will enable you to *give* more to others.

God *always* answers prayer. It is only our own weakness, stubbornness, obtuseness, cynicism—call it what you will—that keeps us from recognizing and benefiting from prayer.

Now the power of prayer is virtually unlimited. Prayer should consist, first of all, of sincere thanks for the blessings that you enjoy. Then, for strength, wisdom and courage to enable one to give more to his fellow man, to help them in turn to acquire a stronger measure of guidance, direction, strength, hope and courage. Include a *specific request for additional knowledge of God's will and the strength, courage and wisdom to carry it out.* These **are the principal ingredients. Do not ask for favors. You ask for** the ability to give more and more so that when it becomes time to leave this earth, you've left it a better place than you found it. The interesting, very practical and simple thing about this is *the more you give, the more you get!!* The more you build people, the more you are built. This is a fundamental fact and I have stated it categorically and dogmatically. I want you to accept it in that way.

Many ministers achieve mediocre success at best by focusing only on what the members of their congregation can do to achieve salvation *for themselves.* Many of these mediocre ministers can become *great* ministers if they can effectively help such members to clearly see how much more they can contribute, give and build. The simple fact is that many capable business and professional people ignore the plea of the evangelist because they simply aren't that *self-centered.* Besides, they rationalize that they can always be shrived at the eleventh hour. But, show these people how much more they can *achieve* and *accomplish because* of a new and vibrant spirit and watch what happens.

For a life of ebullience, fulfillment and power, it is essential that you understand the Principle which towers above all others in this book:

> "We should not and cannot experience optimum success if we consider ourselves to be repositories of God's love. We must be dynamic and passionate instruments for exemplifying and transmitting his love. To do less is to drift gradually toward intellectual and emotional sterility."

The only way that we can truly build deep, sustaining confidence, is to test and practice the use of the principles of tough-minded living on real problems. We can sit in a library and read every book that exists on positive thinking or on tough-minded living or on problem-solving and this will do us very little good until we encounter problems; just as the weight lifter, just as the would-be body-builder will develop no muscle at all by simply sitting and looking at a set of barbells; just as the would-be singer can gain nothing by simply studying music and never exercising the voice. In just this way, we cannot add to this toughness and the strength of our minds by simply reading about what we should do until we are faced with some taxing, stretching requirements to develop this new muscle of the mind. Again, let me use the example of the athlete: the man who wants to be a good pole vaulter, who stands and contemplates that high bar, sets it at about ten feet, grips his bamboo pole and then stands there in the sun and reads all the material he can find about pole-vaulting —this man will never get over that bar. If he's a beginner and he sets that bar up there at ten feet, he'll probably knock it off dozens and dozens of times. But only in that way will he build up the proper muscle, the proper coordination, the proper confidence to ultimately clear that bar.

For this precise reason, then, we must *seek out* problems *and convert them to challenges!* We need to welcome problems with arms open. Embrace them because this can well be some of the finest parts of living. Many older people look back on the years they spent wondering how they would meet the expenses of raising a family, coping with the problems, the illnesses—in some instances the vexations of their children—they look back now and think "those were the most developmental, the most rewarding, the most wonderful years of my life. If I could only have recognized it then."

What they're saying in effect is that they should have welcomed problems. Encountering a steady stream of problems day after day made their lives warm and meaningful. It gave them confidence. It helped insure that their later years would be years of serenity. Welcome problems, reach out for them, charge in to them and convert them in your mind immediately to challenges. The negative way to look at a problem is to think of it as a problem. Search it out, isolate it as a problem, then in your mind convert it to a challenge, determine the steps that you will need to surmount it just as the pole-vaulter needs to first determine steps and then work at it. Only in this way do you develop the skill, the coordination, the mind, the muscle and the confidence to really get it done.

Steps for Accomplishment

1. Conduct the seven-day experiment outlined on pages 51-53. At the end of the week continue for 14, 21, 28 days. Continue it for the rest of your life.

2. Use the mirror frequently for self-improvement purposes.
    A. Determine the person you want to be.
    B. Repeatedly become that person in front of the mirror.
    C. Ultimately—you will become that person.

3. Set your life goals; then break them up into yearly, monthly and daily bite-size goals. It is accomplishment that builds self-confidence—and these bite-size goals can be readily accomplished.

4. Whenever you are prone to use the words "I can't"—strike off the "t" and see how the words "I can" can change your life.

5. You become what you say—talk successfully. Use emotional positive words in your talking. Avoid a vocabulary of morbid negative words.

6. Recognize that true faith in self (self-confidence, positiveness, etc.) is not possible without a faith in the Almighty. Continually develop your personal religious faith.

7. All other techniques are superficial unless the power of prayer is being practiced.

8. Pray only for what you have the right to expect, and expect only what you have the right to pray for.

Think like a man of action and act like a man of thought.

HENRI BERGSON

4 TO BE A COURAGEOUS "TOUGH-MINDED" PERSON OF ACTION

Internal Fibre—Needed to Fill a Bigger Mold

You have observed children and young adults not venturing into unfamiliar activities for fear of failure in the eyes of their companions. A mature adult, however, must realize that to "fill a bigger mold" you must have the courage to constantly try new things.

Lyndall Urwick, a respected authority on business management, has said that an executive must have courage; other necessary criteria can be taught. "Courage," he says, "is in some degree a matter of facing dangers and learning that, if faced, they become less intimidating."

Eleanor Roosevelt in her book *You Learn by Living* (Harper, 1960) does an excellent job of explaining it in this way:

> The encouraging thing is that every time you meet a situation, though you may think at the time it is an impossibility and you go through the tortures of the damned, once you have met it and lived through it you find that forever after you are freer than you ever were before. If you can live through this you can live through anything. You gain strength, courage, and confidence by every experience in which you really stop to look fear in the face. You are able to say to yourself, 'I lived through this horror. I can take the next thing that comes along.' The danger lies in refusing to face the fear, in not daring to come to grips with it. If you fail anywhere along the line it will take away your confidence. You must make yourself succeed every time. You must do the thing you think you cannot do.

This type of internal fiber is a necessity for tough-minded individuals who wish to live a successful and happy life. The truly tough-minded person possesses courage, logic, guts and the power to love.

Love—Powerful, Durable and Tough

Love is the most powerful, durable, and tough of all emotions. The General who uses his rank to chew out, fire, or petrify a Major is not using any type of real strength; he's got the rank and all it takes is an active tongue. In short, it takes no brains and no guts to simply focus in on the weaknesses of another person when you have the rank on them. Recognize this and if you've been preening yourself on being tough-minded because you give people a hard time, scathingly cut them up and make them feel small, recognize that you are just the reverse. You've been indulging in hate which is the most weak and meaningless emotion that any person is capable of.

What do you feel when you get a good idea and someone starts asking you questions designed specifically to uncover what's *wrong* with it? How do you feel when you have given a person some advice and this advice is based only on discussion of what he has done *wrong* or on his *weaknesses?* You felt much *bigger*, much *better* and in every instance you accomplished more when you built on that person's strengths instead of focusing on his weaknesses. So recognize that anybody—and I mean anybody—can scurry through life as a little person indulging in vituperation, in insults, in gossip, in sarcasm, in cynicism, in all of the little innuendoes which add up to one thing—hate. Rid yourself once and for all of every manifestation of hate and you will move very rapidly toward the process which we call growth and success.

Hate—Weak, Rigid and Destructive

If you were to go out into the city tomorrow and round up the fifty most unsuccessful people and get them into a big room (we're not talking about the kind of clothing the person wears or the kind of money they have in the bank; we're talking about the person who feels whipped and exploited by life), you might recruit some of them from Skid Row, some from front offices, some from the ranks of the retired. You might even recruit some from the ministry, the legal profession, or the teaching profession.

But if you were to pick out the fifty most unsuccessful people, put them in a large room and ask them what they are against, I will say unequivocally that they could fill a very long list of what they were *against*. So also, such individuals would be hard put to write down, without equivocation, fifteen or twenty things that they were *for*—because the tangible, day-to-day expression of hate is based upon what the individual is *against*. Many of these people would draw back in shock and sound appalled at the idea that they have hate in their souls, their minds, and their hearts. They say they are against evil, they are against sin, they are against illicit sex, they are against crooked government, and so on. How much easier, helpful and effective it would be if they would state that they are not against sin, but *for* virtue, not against crooked politics, but *for* sound government, not against illicit sex, but *for* sound, sanctified, married love. The person who is able to convert all of his "againsts" to "fors" is the person who is also making significant and substantial progress in converting all of his hate feelings to love feelings. Some reviewers of the world scene have stated that weariness or fatigue are the most prevalent conditions today. Did you know that *one burst of negative anger is more fatiguing than an average day of work?*

Making Things Happen
There are some very specific and distinct techniques for making things happen. We often say "Wishing won't make it so"—and of course this is painfully true in many instances. There are two very key words in the process of making things happen and these two words are *involvement* and *commitment*. If you want to make things happen you have to work through people because management of any kind, whether it's management of a home, a service station or a multi-million dollar company, is the process of developing people and making things happen through and by people.

This is analogous to our method of government, which is government of the people, by the people, and for the people. Now, our democratic form of government cannot work at its optimum or even close to it unless we have people *involved* in the selection of their representatives—*involved* in the point of view and the type of legislation that the particular representatives develop and push through Congress—and people *committed* to the principles which govern our country, *committed* to the representatives we have voted for and selected after appropriate *involvement* with them. Getting a piece of work done at home, in the office, or in the shop, must work just the same way, since we work with and through people. The people who are going to get a piece of work done which we delegate to them must have a chance to apply and provide some opinions; they must have some *involvement* in this decision. Once the involvement has taken place (if you are in a decision-making capacity and you and only you can make that decision) then you must illustrate to the people who work for you *commitment.*

So, the way to make things happen is to determine what you want done, based upon the principles and philosophy that you have, and the requirement of that particular job, incident, or situation. Then make sure the people who are trying to have a hand in this have an opportunity to be heard, an opportunity to share their actual on-the-firing-line experience. In many instances we are overlooking a very vital and important source of contribution with many of our employees because we don't let them have a hand in the preparation for the decision. Thus, they feel no commitment to that decision; thus, we achieve mediocre success in making things happen.

I believe it could be stated emphatically that no truly successful man ever became that way without doing a great many things that he feared to do, but had the courage to do in spite of fear. We have seen some pretty nondescript, average, mediocre people become tough-minded, powerful and successful by making a complete list of all of the things that they fear, exploring in detail the anatomy of their fear, finding out precisely what it is and, in most instances, they find that the very thing that they fear holds no fear at all, *once they have confronted it, looked at it squarely, and discovered that the only thing that they feared was the fear that they would fear.* This sounds amazingly simple because it is; but it is amazingly powerful. Set down an actual list of everything that you fear and why you fear them, when you fear them, where, how, with, from and by whom? In this way you'll discover the feeling of growth and confidence that can surely come from targeting the things you fear and doing them.

It is impossible to get something accomplished without starting—but so many people never start because of fear of failure. The words that William Shakespeare gave to Julius Caesar are certainly appropriate in this regard. "Cowards die many times before their death—the valiant never taste of death, but once."

Some physicians, we're told, claim that the measure of a top surgeon is that "he cuts fast and deep—and gets out quick." This is a good analogy for other walks of life. The surgeon who is unsure of himself can cut a little bit at a time and butcher his patient. The individual can do the same thing to his life in piecemeal, unsure steps.

Knowledge into Action

Perhaps one of the most misunderstood concepts in America today is the belief that knowledge is learning, that the process of assimilating information will automatically result in real learning. Until an individual discovers that this is not so, he has a difficult time translating knowledge into action because he may, again, want to follow the procedure of the "bland leading the bland." He may feel that the secret of success is simply a great deal of book learning, a great deal of knowledge which he absorbs from all those around him. But simply absorbing knowledge from others doesn't really add very much to your total stature; it doesn't really add very much to your total impact: your total capacity for successful living. Until you convert this knowledge into a condition which is reflected in what you actually *do* and *say* and how you *live*, then you have not learned, because learning is very simply and basically defined as the "modification of behavior." So, insist, then, that the knowledge be converted into some type of behavior which has some impact on your relations with your family or on your job, on the particular goals toward which you are striving in life. Otherwise, you can spend that time much more wisely in pursuing a different kind of knowledge.

The Self-Starter

What's the difference between the person who knows how to start himself and the person who feels he must rely on somebody else to start him toward certain tasks and assignments? It can be boiled down simply to this: The self-starter has a lesser amount of fear of the consequences. Thus, he sets out to get some action accomplished, to get a program accomplished. The person who seems to be hampered by a ballast of inertia and doubt and fear has to be pushed. He has to be jogged a little bit. So we're talking here, again, about how to eradicate *fear*.

There are two basic, pervasive ways to eliminate fear in our society—to cultivate a deep understanding of two documents, two sources encompassing many documents: one is the New Testament and the other is the Constitution of the United States. A thorough examination of the Constitution shows that there is no basis in this country of ours for economic fear if the true nature of the Constitution is understood and applied in a tough-minded and passionate way. Of much more significance, a thorough analysis, discussion, and reflection of all of the basic truths covered in the New Testament show that there is ample provision made for survival, for the pleasant and abundant functioning and living of the individual who truly believes and knows how to control and direct these truths to get a job done. So, if you aspire to be a real self-starter, return to the list of things that you fear. Recognize that you can rapidly move toward becoming a real self-starter in direct proportion to your ability—to your progress—in eliminating all of the items which you fear, the items which still appear to be roadblocks to swift, sure, dynamic patterns of action. Once again, determine what you are for. What you stand for is the whole foundation for courage. Believe deep enough and passionately enough in something and you will be moved to take action.

Courage—Superficial or Deep Conviction

Man does not live by bread alone. One of the most important requirements for a powerful life is courage—courage to cast out of your mind and your life all roadblocks to the dynamic use and renewal of physical and mental energy. Many "personality experts" suggest a number of techniques whereby you can transmit to others the image that you are successful simply by asking about their health, by deferring to them, by making them feel "good" by the manner in which you look at them, by the manner in which you shake their hand, by the clothes which you wear and things of this kind. This type of behavior can definitely help you succeed. But, true success will always elude you unless you dig deep into your reservoir and ensure that you have fortified your spirit with *system,* with *order,* with *values,* with *beliefs,* with *experience,* with the whole warp and weave of the fabric of self-belief, and with a genuine desire to lift your head high above the dull, mundane, plodding habit of "literal" living.

Lloyd C. Douglas in his great book *The Living Faith* (Houghton Mifflin Company) says, "You cannot rub courage into a man from the outside with 'personality' improvements any more than you can rub arthritis out of a man with liniment. You may set up a temporary counterirritant that will distract his attention from his disability, but that is all. The treatment gives no promise of permanent aid. You can apply an electrode to the sciatic nerve of a dead frog so that he will kick a few times in a very lifelike manner, but the dead frog in the long run is a lost cause. You cannot make a man permanently hopeful by inviting him to join in singing, 'Pack Up Your Troubles In Your Old Kit Bag and Smile'; nor does it help him to put up the month's business in black ink by singing 'Happy Days Are Here Again.' We have relied too heavily on these brief intoxicants to furnish our optimism."

But here he says what must be done: "To the achievement of hope a man must become assured that he is living in a universe that is entirely solvent and time-worthy. In the hands of a God to whose own interest it is that the universe shall preserve its integrity. He must lay hold upon the conviction that the divine urge of which he is conscious is an organic part of the life of God and that when any one of these divine sparks in human creatures smolders to extinction for sheer neglect, God's power in the universe is impeded by just that much."

Steps for Accomplishment

1. Learn courage by living.
   A. Recognize that you gain confidence and courage every time you meet a situation head-on that you were previously afraid of.
   B. When faced with the situation where you are apprehensive come to grips with it. "You must do the thing you cannot do."
   C. Permanent and lasting courage comes from continually living through experiences where you have done what you thought you could not do.
   D. Constantly try new things that you have not done before.
   E. Forget the word "failure"—fear of it will prevent you from starting things that will never get done—unless you start.
   F. Remember Lyndall Urwick's statement: "Courage is in some degree facing dangers and learning that, if faced, they become less intimidating."

2. To remove fear—
   A. Refuse to let your mistakes harness you. Be grateful that they show you what not to do in the future; so you gain from your experiences.
      (1) Try to learn from every mistake you make.
      (2) Try not to make the same mistake twice.

3. There is no time more favorable to you than right now—take action now.
   A. Taking action will keep you busy—remember there is no greater remedy for tension and fear than hard work.
   B. Develop a mental, physical image of yourself as a trim, courageous person. Emulate this image with a physical development program—chest out and stomach in. Physical fitness is a key to courage.
   C. Courage is synonymous with faith. You must have faith in yourself, in your fellow man and in an Almighty.

You seldom get what you go after unless you know in advance what you want. Indecision has often given an advantage to the other fellow because he did his thinking beforehand.

MAURICE SWITZER

5 The Power to Choose

THE POWER TO MAKE DECISIONS

Perhaps the most precious of all gifts from the Almighty is the *power to choose!!!* This is a human gift that transcends and exceeds every other power that we have been gifted with. The extent, then, to which we use this particular gift in some instances can be a talent, and in others can be a virtual affliction—in the positive thinker it's a talent; it's the golden road to achievement, to success, to total living. To the truly negative thinker, to the defeatist, to the defensive, self-preoccupied individual, this ceases to be a gift and becomes an affliction. The fearful individual begins to back away from what should be a glorious privilege and uses it as a series of demanding, painful obligations. Here, I think, we can see in the most practical way possible the down-to-earth, every-day importance of positive thinking and acting as opposed to negative and defeatist thinking and acting.

Let me review this. First of all, the power to choose is the most powerful gift we possess. Second, if we have developed and are developing positive patterns of behavior, positive attitudes, it can be a series of wonderful and uplifting *privileges*. If we have developed a fear and negative-oriented pattern of behavior, we then have to look for a life filled with a series of obligations that we feel are forced upon us by a cold, callous world.

Think with Power and Unity

We could talk at great length about the mechanics (the sequential process of making decisions) and would probably contribute very little to the real wisdom needed to make decisions in this kaleidoscopic, ever-changing aerospace age if we did not include adequate provisions for gaining total perspective. These are fancy words, but let's see what they mean. Think with power and unity. This means that the power of decision, the power of applied wisdom comes from values which charge the battery, which enrich the mind, which toughen and add substance and fibre to the ability to face difficult decisions and make them regardless of immediate consequences.

By unity we mean the kind of updated, space-age executive who is able to see the essential unity between the world around him in its relationship with his country and to the company walls which surround him. He must then be able to see the unity of life in this modern world, and this—of necessity—requires that he rigorously reject any considerations of the past based upon outdated or stereotyped concepts of what people really are. In making decisions he must recognize that undeveloped nations which may be affected by his particular business decision contain the same individuals with dignity and needs, goals and desires, that we find right here in our own part of the country. He must face these decisions because of the vastly-increased communications in this small, spinning planet of ours; he must see the impact that one fairly major decision has upon many segments of the rest of the world and apply to it the results of his wisdom, not only of his pure, crisp intellect.

Now, this may sound a little bit involved at this point. Let's boil it down and see what we're really saying. This means that the man sitting at a desk is faced with a comprehensive report from his computer which shows what his competitor is doing, what his current share of the market is and how his competitors in foreign countries are doing—this gives him the raw data, the raw stuff, the basic decision-making data which is considered adequate in many companies at the present time. After this, then, recognize the fundamental fact that management is the development of people, not the direction of things and then we realize that a decision is only going to be as good as the quality of the mind which makes it. Recognize, further, that the mind is capable, informed and has depth and wisdom only if it sees its place in connection with the other minds, not only in the company, the community, the state, the country, but the world. This total conception of unity and power gives to one a kind of wisdom that makes for decisions that are truly successful.

Make Your Values Work for You

Decisions are the stuff of life. Decisions are the product of a mind. *The total mind is a product of its individual values.* Probably nothing can be more practical than uncovering, discovering and using values—values that have to do with excellence, with the Creator, with our Constitution, with the impact of Supreme Court decisions, with an awareness of the Gettysburg Address, The Declaration of Independence, the Emancipation Proclamation—all of the great manifestos of American history which have a daily, urgent, pervasive impact on the operation of our lives. You might say, for instance, what on earth does the Emancipation Proclamation, issued many years ago, have to do with a business decision today? You have only to pick up the headlines of any newspaper or listen for a moment to any news broadcast and you will quickly perceive that one of the most pressing, serious, overriding problems of America today is the problem of Negro relations and its impingement upon the successful operation of a business or of any enterprise. This was triggered off by the Emancipation Proclamation, the great American manifesto which set the legal framework and showed a cultural lag that is part of the greatest lags of all time. This showed that the minds of men and the values which make up those minds were way behind the legal framework which was enacted by the Supreme Court of that day.

Mistakes Within Reason

Now any preoccupation with mistakes can sound negative, like a focus on weaknesses instead of strengths, but we must recognize even in a very realistic, positive, strength-oriented view that in the final analysis people are all human. We all have frailties, we all make mistakes, and we must be allowed to make mistakes within reason. When somebody makes a mistake that bothers you and seems to thwart your plan or seems to be in some way an affront to you, you will gain absolutely nothing by zeroing in on their weaknesses, dwelling on that mistake, not letting them forget it. This will maximize very definitely the possibility that they will continue to make not only that mistake but other mistakes, because they start operating under the influence of fear instead of enthusiasm, of push instead of pull, of force instead of direction. So, in a creative climate within the home, within the community or within a business, recognize that it is positive and it is realistic that all people make some mistakes. When a person makes a mistake, review with them what it is; let him know that you know what it is, then forget about it and concentrate only upon what he can do about it.

If you are unrealistic enough, you mistake the meaning of positive thinking to the extent that you say, "I will have no mistakes in this organization or in this home," which makes you guilty of a truly negative behavior pattern. So recognize, as we point out from time to time, that the truly positive thinker is first of all a very realistic thinker and he recognizes the weaknesses which do exist in a situation, but he builds and concentrates and devotes his time and energy only to the strengths that exist, with the full knowledge that this is the one best and pervasive way to eliminate their weaknesses.

Steps for Accomplishment

1. Are your senses needle sharp? Is your mind at razor's edge? It's going to take all you have to see the awesome potential impact of the thought I'm going to advance here. Think now!

    Whether you consider him as a great teacher or as Christ, imagine that Jesus arrived in a busy downtown business area at 9:00 A.M. next Monday in a business suit and crew cut. What would he say? How would he act? How would he react? Try the challenging and somewhat unsettling series of questions on the following page.

THE SITUATION	WHAT WOULD JESUS DO?	WHAT WOULD YOU DO?
A. A child falls in front of an automobile.		
B. A competitor calls you a yellow S.O.B.		
C. You're offered complete financial security to spend the rest of your life in total leisure.		
D. You are locked in a room with a group of lepers.		
E. You are told your job depends upon attending a cocktail party composed of people whom you virtually despise.		
F. You say you are chronically tired.		
G. You just got fired.		
H. Your wife (or husband) has just angrily stated that all love for you has fled.		
I. You have just inherited one million dollars.		

THE SITUATION	WHAT WOULD JESUS DO?	WHAT WOULD YOU DO?
J. Your house has burned down.		
K. Your closest friend dies unexpectedly.		
L. You are called "ugly, disgusting and stupid."		
M. You are called "handsome, charming, fascinating and incomparable."		
N. You've just become president of your company.		
O. You've just been demoted to the most insignificant job you can think of.		
P. The elevator is stuck between floors and you are two hours late for an important engagement.		
Q. (Add some more for yourself and answer them with complete honesty.)		

Every great and commanding movement in the annals of the world is the triumph of enthusiasm. Nothing great was ever accomplished without it.

—EMERSON

6 Enthusiasm, Zeal and Fervor

THE CONTAGION OF PASSIONATE ENTHUSIASM

Enthusiasm is defined by Webster in the following manner—"to be inspired or possessed by the God, divine inspiration or possession, ecstasy, transport, ardent zeal or interest, fervor." The Greek definition of enthusiasm is "God within." And this is actually what we are talking about. It has become popular in certain circles to label the word "enthusiasm" as being trite. They say it's corny to talk about enthusiasm and to label certain leaders of the basic mental attitude called enthusiasm as "Knute Rockne type locker room orators." The vast majority of Americans today have had a great tendency to move around under a cloud of lack-luster enthusiasm. Somehow it has come to seem sophisticated to give a somewhat dispirited, diffident, listless or jaded reaction to anybody who brings up an idea with a bright eye and a flushed cheek and say, "Don't be corny." Somehow the feeling has developed that it is sophisticated to express a certain amount of jaundiced cynicism, to question, to query, to seek reassurance before putting some energy into a particular cause. This was never part of nature's plan. Man was intended to walk upright, not only physically, but with his mind, heart and spirit —questing, growing, changing until the day he dies, and this can only be done through developing and using *enthusiasm!!!!*

Drudgery Depends on Attitude

Let's take a look at what the word drudgery means. Drudgery is defined as "act of drudging, ignoble or wearisome toil." A drudge is defined as "to perform menial work, hence to toil at any difficult and monotonous task, one who drudges a hack." It's a little upsetting to concede, but I think we must face the fact that the large majority of Americans today do consider a good bit of their work as being drudgery. Many consider the day-to-day responsibilities of marriage as drudgery. Many consider the whole process of living, hour-by-hour, day-by-day, week-by-week, a process of drudgery, wearisome, toilsome, and the ironic, basic and important thing is that everything we do actually becomes drudgery when our attitude pushes us in this direction. *We become what we say.* Of course this has been established. We also become what we *think*. And if we think that life is full of drudgery, if we think our work is full of drudgery, if we think that going to a gala social occasion is going to be drudgery, you can certainly count on the fact that it's going to be drudgery. So we have to back off and overhaul basic attitudes. Are we in life to have some fun, are we in life to achieve something, do we walk through this life in the process of building, or are we drifting more and more into a cocoon, a self-preoccupa-

THE CONTAGION OF PASSIONATE ENTHUSIASM   81

tion where we seem in effect to return to the womb and cuddle up looking for vitality, comfort and warmth to our own body and our own self? This can most certainly make life a series of toilsome wearisome tasks, because we do not reach out and benefit from the electric charges of other people's personalities, the charges which are magnified and increased by the electrons, protons and molecules that we project, with which we build and nurture other people's minds. The more we give to them, the more they give to us, and the problem of drudgery drifts rather readily into the past. Do you have the courage, do you have the brains?

We can virtually sentence ourself to a lifetime of drudgery; of patient, diffident, long-suffering lack lustre living, or we can cast these shackles off. We can break the shell, we can emerge with a bang from the cloak of drudgery if we simply *decide* to. All too many of us approach the matter of living in a dogged way. We've got to *get through* the day, we've got to *get through* the business conference at lunch, we've got to *get through* the housework in the morning, we've got to *get through* the weekend, we look upon life as a series of problems, not challenges. The difference might seem to be minute, but the difference is vital. The way in which you address yourself to this rare and beautiful privilege of living will determine completely what you do with it. Are you going to simply react to your environment? React to your life? Or, are you going to get your life to react to you? Are you the slave of your soul or are you its master? Only *you* can make that decision. The most important thing is that you start off the morning by pumping into yourself some reason for anticipating the unfolding of the day. You may have to reach out. You may have to initially do a good bit of straining. And, no matter how much you develop over the years, you will still, perhaps, have moments when you have to reach deep into your own reservoir and to do a little spiritual engineering. This means you must rig up and put together some of the spiritual fiber that makes your life unique; that enables you to address your mind, heart and spirit to converting every problem to a challenge, every *against* to a *for*, every *negativism* to a *positivism*, every *fear* to a *confidence*, every *failure* to a *triumph*.

It *can* be done, but the only way it can be done is to rigorously strike the "T" off of the word can't.

Vitality and Vigor

Let's take a look now at what the word vital means. It is defined as follows: "Of, pertaining to, or existent as a manifestation of life. Vital functions or energy. Essential to the continuance of life or full physical vigor. Necessary to life, as wounded in a vital part. Vital blood. Vital personality. Fatal, mortal, as a vital wound. Fundamentally effecting the continuation, value, efficiency or the like of anything." Vitality means state or quality of being vital, life, animate, existence, the principle of life. If we want to experience vitality and its natural result, which is vigor, we have to again get down to the basic principles. What is it then in the most basic analysis that gives us vitality, that gives us a higher measure of searching, pulsing vital life? The mind and the body are both saturated, controlled and influenced by the spirit, but the body first of all must be a healthy temple for a healthy mind to develop. At the same time in a sort of servo-mechanism manner the body can only become truly healthy and experience full growth and vigor as a product of a mind which focuses on positives, on things that can be done, on achievement, on building, on accomplishment. A mind that rigidly rejects the kind of considerations, the kind of thoughts, attitudes, or fears that have to do with losing, that have to do with failure, that have to do with the weaknesses of a situation or the weaknesses of others. The vital mind in a vital life has no time, absolutely no time, for a concentration or focus on the negativist and the loser. The vital person knows that the only way he can become increasingly vital is to give of his vitality to others and to increase their vitality, thus setting up a cross mechanism, a cross interchange of electronic stimulation which makes of life something truly worth while.

Here's a fascinating little experiment. Take a week of vacation. Lie around all week, don't shave, feel real sloppy—*relax!* Then on

Sunday, get up early, shave, shower and go to church. Notice a difference? Of course you will. You are actually more rested, refreshed and vitalized on Sunday afternoon than you were any other time during the week. One reason for this is because you round out the vital balance of Work, Love, Play and Worship (WLPW).

Contagious Enthusiasm—Positive Emotion

The term contagious basically means spreading from one to another. Time and again executives at various levels have complained that the enthusiasm among their subordinates was not what it should be. Much of the time this executive simply has to take a close look at himself and ask himself whether he is insuring that his own enthusiasm is strong enough, bubbling enough, obvious enough that it literally leaps from him to others. He must look enthusiastic, sound enthusiastic, walk tall, walk with his chest out, put some vibrancy and power and force into his voice. Make sure that every emotion that stimulates the emoting or speaking that he does is based upon a positive type of motivation. This is the only way to make sure that enthusiasm is truly contagious.

Tough-Mindedness as a Way of Life

We have defined tough-mindedness from time to time, and will continue to, as a quality of mind that is resilient, tough, flexible, pliant, fibrous, that prepares a person for all of the experiences of life whether these be disappointment, triumphs, accomplishments, tragedies. The tough-minded person rises above the particular moment in time when he is hit with a particular problem or disappointment and he tries to see the broad picture. His mind is resilient and is reaching out grasping for new positivism, new faith, new manifestations of the Creator, new reasons for hope, and thus he seldom ever finds himself in the pit of despair or subject to peaks and valleys in emotion such as many people in our current society do. This person is experiencing tough-mindedness, he is making it a way of life because he has learned to *get out of himself,* to virtually exist in the thoughts, minds and emotions of others. This in no way means that he is sacrificing or playing down his own dignity and his own self-hood. This man is not encouraging the development of a condition of anonymity, but he finds that the more he gives, the more he projects, the more surely his own personality becomes defined, the more sharply etched it is in terms of its content, its quality. In short, the more a person helps other people to understand themselves with dedication, with thoroughness, with devotion, the more surely that man will understand himself. So when you hear the "lost soul," and perhaps from time to time you have said this to yourself as you look in the mirror or as you lie in the dark uttering a silent forlorn thought, the phrase "Who am I" comes into your mind. What am I, why am I here, what's life all about, where am I going, where did I come from, what, where, who, how, why?? These are big things in the mind of the person who has not yet achieved full maturity, a full awareness of the juices of life, of the savor and the flavor of abundant and full living. So I repeat, the one best way to find yourself is to help others find themselves through providing them with clear-cut values, encouragement, strength, guidance and uplift. The forlorn lament, excuse or crutch —call it what you will—that many people use to keep from doing a vigorous thing goes as follows: "Who am I after all to try and tell him what to do." "Who am I after all to try and give her guidance or hope at a time like this." This can make a comforting excuse for you not to take the kind of positive action that cracks you out of your shell and enables you to be of real life giving force to other people. Here's who you are. You must see yourself as a creature of God who has a mind and a soul which distinguishes you from all other forms of animal, vegetable and mineral life. You have a mind, you have a soul. You are a unique creation of God. Nobody else on the face of this earth is quite like you. Nobody stands in your way. Nobody stands in the path of total accomplishment, total success, except you. Following are nine attributes of a "little" man. This is the "abominable non-man" that we could do without. If this is the man you see when you look in the mirror, *this is the kind of personality you can do without* and I'm sure you'll do something about it. Here is the little man (the abominable no-man):

1. He is wrapped up in himself and his own interests.
2. He has many fears; for example, that people will take advantage of him.
3. He makes the simple seem complex, so it usually is.
4. He thinks of the easy as difficult, and the difficult as impossible. Again, they usually are.
5. He thinks in terms of actions rather than end results.
6. He accepts others' ideas with reluctance, if at all. When he does he may represent them as his own.
7. He often wants something for nothing.
8. He is critical of others' weaknesses and seldom acknowledges their strengths.
9. He lacks a real and abiding faith in himself, in God, or in anyone else.

Think and Speak with Passion

What about this? Haven't we been told that whenever we show overt passion that we are somehow violating some moral or legal law, that we should sublimate these passions, that we should be glacial, that we should be bland, that we should be neutral, that we should keep from becoming a victim of our emotions? Let's back off and take a real long look at this and recognize that the only time, the only way in which we can ultimately be in almost complete control of our emotions is to recognize that we are going to have them if we are leading a meaningful and full, vital life. The need for love, the need for sex, the need for certain emotions that approximate wrath, for instance, is very human and natural for a person to feel toward immoral or unworthy acts on the part of himself or others. These are emotions that were given to us. These are emotions that are a part of us and we cannot deny them. When we lock them up within us, seek to sublimate them, seek to hide them, we simply begin to build poison within us which causes ulcers, various aspects of nervous degeneration, breakdowns, hysteria, and so on. So let's take a good look at these emotions. Let's recognize that we have them and then learn to use them with feeling, but recognize that the key thing is that we use them to *create*, to *build*, and to *give*, rather than just the reverse. In this way passion can become truly worthwhile.

The Constructive Passions

Constructive passions are listed as four: faith, hope, love, sex. You will note that fear is not mentioned. Anxiety is not mentioned. Envy, worry, defensiveness, hate, sarcasm, cynicism, suspicion—none of these emotions are listed as the constructive passions. Why? Because they are purely and simply destructive.

You are reading this book for one primary purpose, and that is to *build* yourself, to *build* a greater career, to *build* greater confidence, to *build* greater proficiency. Thus, the only passions that we should focus upon and learn to use are the passions which are constructive because only in that way do we completely wash away, destroy, dissolve and forget the destructive passions.

So the constructive passions called Faith, Hope, Love, and Sex should be written down indelibly in your mind. Ask yourself at this point and time—do you have faith that lives *with* you, lives *for* you, breathes new meaning and vitality *into* you twenty-four hours a day? Do you have hope when the chips are down, when all seems dark, when the headlines scream with tragedy, when the storms come, when adversities set in? One particular definition of Hell on Earth is a life without hope. Do you have love? Have you distinguished in your mind between the silly vapid concepts of love associated only with moonlight and roses, with plucking a mandolin and singing the latest hit songs to your loved one? This of course represents a certain passing form of infatuation, of sexual attraction, of boy-meets-girl heat of the moment type of love. The only kind of real love between a man and a woman comes from the absolute unity which comes about (1) mentally and spiritually through the marriage contract which takes place through the church as the particular temple or medium of communication which sanctifies marriage and makes it Holy, this is what welds a couple into one spiritually. (2) The production of children is a tangible outstanding physical testimony to the physical oneness of the marriage partners. Love is defined in the dictionary as "a feeling of strong personal attachment induced by sympathetic understanding or by ties of kinship, ardent affection. The benevolence attributed to God as being like a father's affection for his children also men's adoration of God. Strong liking, fondness, good will as love of learning, love of country, tender and passionate affection for one of the opposite sex, the object of affection, sweetheart, etc." These are of course spontaneous meaningful total symbols or manifestations of the unity of two souls who truly share a strong common love rooted in a deep faith. The modern family that is truly wed in the eyes of the Creator represents a complete oneness. There is no dichotomy, there is no division, they are *one*. When adversity comes, when problems arise, when children are sick, the true marriage pulls closer and closer into one rather than allowing divisive, disturbing influences to creep between them. This simply is not possible when a marriage is properly conceived as being one of *total unity*. Now—interestingly enough, love between a man-for-man, woman-for-woman, worker-for-worker in no way suggests the same kind of ardence, of sexual expression, etc., but you will note in the definition of love given here that there are some truly fine standards or goals for men to strive for in their relationship with their fellow man. This means strong liking, respect, fondness, good will, a desire to help, a feeling of kinship, a sympathetic understanding, a desire to improve. This particular total concept of love is sorely missing in the world today and the readers of this book could become leaders in their respective spheres of life because of the use of this very positive, very strong, very powerful emotion. The strongest emotion on earth.

Sex is listed as the fourth of the constructive passions and sex in its modern connotation still has a long way to go before it measures up to the true nature of sex as outlined by the Bible which is the master architect for all human behavior. Somewhere and somehow a negative, dirty, subversive, dishonorable connotation has grown up so that many people now think that picking up a magazine full of girly pictures and looking at it furtively and lasciviously is somehow connected with sex. *This is simply negative and immature pornography, nothing else.* It has nothing to do with the sanctified, completely honorable, completely normal, completely desirable type of sexual relations that all appropriately married people should enter into with devotion and energy and in a manner totally devoid of apology or distortion.

Passionate Commitment

The great Lutheran pastor, Dr. Louis H. Valbracht, in a message prepared especially for this book says this about passionate enthusiasm and commitment:

> The head of a vaudeville dog act puts it this way: "I never had my dogs play dead because in this day and age the whole audience is doing that."
>
> It is a frightening phenomenon of our day that marketing research and motivational research finally end in addressing advertising messages and radio and TV commercials to the largest audience in the nation.
>
> Who makes up this vast audience? The text of the advertising gives us the obvious answer. They are pointed to the place where the "party's laggin, the party's draggin." It is to people with sluggish livers, nervous headachey depression, sagging appetites, loss of pep or energy; to people who go to bed tired and wake up exhausted; to people who feel limp, lethargic, lusterless, lazy, languid or lifeless. The mood affects every walk of life. University professors speak of the student bodies of their institutions

as silent, dull, and unmoved. They have no strong commitments, no passionate objectives, no idealistic aspirations. One professor speaks of them as "a sodden mass of unmotivated and unmoved flesh."

One Russian newsman, during the Olympic Games, observed to one American sports writer that our American athletes seemed so cool about the approaching events. They acted as though it didn't matter whether they won or lost. What the Russian didn't know was that it might not always be an act. Tragically, it could be a national characteristic in the United States.

Ours is the day when we draw back from fervor. We avoid the contagion of real enthusiasm. We shy away from, and are even suspicious of, passionate commitments. Why?

We have heard the dangers of enthusiasm enumerated:

1. Passion or enthusiasm cripples the critical faculties.
2. Passionate commitment breeds dogmatism and cruelty.
3. Passion can turn a crowd into a mob. Crimes have often been committed by enthusiastic mobs.

But let us say with utter conviction that passion is natural and normal in the human personality. We cannot live fully and completely without it. We are creatures of *feeling*. We cannot live without our emotions, no matter how much trouble we have with them. It is a simple human characteristic that we do not enjoy the company of dull, apathetic persons. We do not enjoy *being* dull, apathetic persons. A young man of my acquaintance broke his engagement to a fine young woman, and gave me as the reason, "I didn't want to live the rest of my life with a woman whose pulse never gets over 76." A line from a TV drama is significant, as the heroine cries out to the hero, "Love me or hate me, but, for God's sake, don't just sit there and ignore me." A wife complained to me, "I wish sometimes that my husband would kiss me as though he were not afraid of mussing my hair." Our culture is conscious of its own lack of passionate commitment to anything.

> "*A soldier with no zest for fighting,*
> *An author with no zeal for writing,*
> *An architect without a plan,*
> *The prototype of modern man.*"

Despite the dangers of enthusiasm and passionate commitment, it remains the greatest prerequisite for abundant living. It is an absolute necessity in every great effort or achievement. Emerson was as cold blooded a thinker as this nation ever produced, and yet he said: "Every great and commandant triumph in the annals of the world is the triumph of enthusiasm." Even in his sober treatise on ethics he comes up with this one: "No virtue is safe that is not enthusiastic."

A good citizen must have a passionate love for his country—an enthusiasm for her life, her culture and her institutions—if he is to be alert to her unsolved problems and her unmet needs. An artist must have a burning passion to say something with his art that has not been said before, or in a way which has not been said previously.

Over the centuries Christianity has grown through the contagious, passionate commitments of individual Christians. St. John the Divine, writing to the church at Laodicea, passionately castigates that church in the book of Revelations: "I know your works, you are neither cold nor hot and therefore I will spew you out of my mouth."

Johannes Weiss in his book *The History of Primitive Christianity* says: "A tempestuous enthusiasm, an overwhelming intensity of feeling, an immediate awareness of the presence of God, an incomparable sense of power and an irresistible control over the will and inner spirit and even the physical conditions of other men—these are ineradicable features of historic early Christianity."

Once a young deacon preached a trial sermon for Archbishop Temple. When he finished he hastened to the good bishop with the question: "Well, Sir, will that do?" Temple asked the devastating question, "Do what?"

One stodgy preacher was told to put more fire in his sermons or more sermons in the fire.

Reformer Martin Luther knew the wonder of flaming conviction. He had no patience with lukewarmness. Once he said: "I say one thing boldly and freely, that nobody is nearer to God than those who hate and deny him, and he has no more dear children than these."

That's an astounding statement. What did he mean? There is something absolute about faith that demands everything or nothing. If it is genuine, it is everything. It touches everything, it transforms everything. If it is thrown into question everything is thrown into question: all of life is at stake.

That's what Luther is saying. The passionate unbeliever who hates and denies God may be all wrong in his ideas, but at least he takes God seriously. He's not just a mere unbeliever, he's an antibeliever whose whole life is wrestling with God's spirit. His whole mind is preoccupied with the problem of faith. Whatever else he may do, he doesn't take God for granted. He does not commit the ultimate sin of indifference. For that reason Luther says he's near to God and dear to him. Someone has said that the greatest sin against a human being is not to hate him, but to ignore him. Just so with God. Not unbelief, but indifference; not atheism, but taking God for granted is the ultimate sin. Look at the passionate denier, and you see the Holy Spirit at work.

Nietzsche, the German philosopher was an atheist. But he was an atheist because he was infuriated with the utter insipidity of the Christianity of his time. Mockingly, passionately, he denounced its stodginess, its superficiality, its sentimentality. With blinding anger he exposed the degradation of faith into the conventional sanctification of conventional mediocrity.

"Who takes God seriously?" he asked. Because he could find no one who did, he said: "God is dead."

What holds true of our religious faith holds true in every facet of human existence. Without passionate commitment, energy, intelligence, and talent are not brought to bear upon any problem. The warming light of the sun gathered together by a magnifying glass and concentrated at a single point can liquefy steel. Eleven little men on a football team, with the passionate desire to win, can give away 40 pounds a man and still defeat an opponent who is uncommitted to victory. A relative handful of continental troops with a passionate desire for liberty defeated the armed might of George III and the British Empire. It is a simple truism that passionate commitment to a cause provides a person with almost unbelievable physical strength.

To save a precious, newly purchased piano, two men carried the heavy instrument up a narrow stairway in the face of a swift-rising flood. It took six men to carry the piano down the stairs after the waters had receded.

A wise salesmanager, after a long explanation of the features, values, advantages and superiority of an appliance, asked the sales force: "Do you all understand it?" There were no questions. Then he asked the much more relevant question, "Do you all believe it?" Without that passionate commitment the sales effort would be in vain.

Essentially however, the real thrill of passionate commitment is a sense of personal *aliveness*. Our senses are needle sharp. Our intelligence cuts with a razor edge. Boundless energy flows into our physical frame, and we are inspired by the faith that can move mountains. Out of this seething cauldron of unleashed power effervesces into the total being of a man the glorious joy of living—fully, richly, and abundantly.

Criticism—Positive or Futile

And now, last of all in the considerations involved in developing enthusiasm, how do you go about criticizing people. When you are asked to evaluate or give an opinion of somebody's performance on the stage, in the athletic gym, at work, what do you do? Do you automatically assume that this means you should look for something wrong so that you can present it either cheerfully or cynically, or do you recognize the true meaning of criticism which simply means *to enlighten so that performance may improve?*

It is one of the great mistakes of our current society, our current way of life, that we assume that criticism means to point out weaknesses. Criticism was never fundamentally intended for this purpose. Criticism means to provide information which will enable the individual receiving that criticism to make better use of his existing talents and strengths.

Passionate Enthusiam

1. *Passionate Enthusiasm* is the outward image of internal beliefs and values. Others will recognize you as a person who knows

what he stands for and has sincere positive values and beliefs.
2. *Passionate Enthusiasm* is contagious. You provide leadership in changing behavior and goals of others in their emulation of your spirit and zest.
3. *Passionate Enthusiasm* develops vigor. When you have developed basic philosophies, principles and goals, and you pursue these with passion you find that you have extensive energy and vigor, you are not losing strength through frustration and quandary.
4. *Passionate Enthusiasm* accomplishes results. Because the passionate person has set goals and organized his plans, and sells with passion the job gets done. The "wheelspinner, pop gun" enthusiast is left waiting at the gate because his enthusiasm is usually superficial.
5. The Passionate Person is just the reverse of the Passive Putterer.

Dare To Live With Passionate Enthusiasm!

Steps for Accomplishment

1. Have you developed internal values and beliefs? Let people know what they are—get excited about them.
2. Find someone who does not have firm beliefs and try to persuade him to adopt yours. Don't argue or belittle—be persuasive with enthusiam.
3. Make a commitment to yourself to double the amount of enthusiasm you put into life and work.
4. Force yourself to act enthusiastic. Force yourself to show passion. This way through practice you will become passionately enthusiastic.

A man generally has two reasons for doing a thing; one that sounds good, and a real one.

J. PIERPONT MORGAN

7

The Power of Projection
—Strengths or Weaknesses

UNDERSTANDING HUMAN BEHAVIOR

Not too long ago an eminent psychologist was presenting a day of lectures and discussion to a major professional group. Late in the afternoon someone asked him, "How can I keep from reacting with dislike or with suspicion to people who work with me when I feel that I have done my best to help them, but they seem to persist in being hateful, reluctant, negligent, etc. I am *really concerned* about this. I mean well but I do find myself getting disturbed at some of these people and I want to know what to do about it." The answer was this: "Until you learn to love yourself it is impossible to love others,—until you learn that you have, that you possess, a number of real strengths, a number of real talents, a number of real achievements, it is virtually impossible for you to help other people achieve greater things, to grow, to mature, to improve." Therefore the number of people we see who seem to annoy us, who seem to disturb us, are usually reflections of the imperfections we see in ourselves. This is why we place great emphasis, why we urge strongly again and again, to understand yourselves and to focus on your strengths, not on your weaknesses, because all of us are painfully aware of these weaknesses anyway. Although most of us are pretty well informed on what our weaknesses are, unless we know what our strengths are we cannot improve them, we cannot use them, we cannot unify and organize them to get real things done. The interesting, although simple, fact is that our *weaknesses* will steadily dissolve and disappear once we begin to make effective and steady use of our *strengths*. So first we must spell out, understand, memorize and learn to use our strengths so that they keep increasing, so they will enable us to overcome obstacles and build our confidence because this is the only real, lasting and meaningful way to develop an evermore strengthening, evermore pleasant, evermore harmonious picture of those around us.

If we know we are strong we will recognize strength in others. If we think we are weak, we are going to focus on the weakness of others. There is perhaps one of the greatest challenges that you have in the life which will stretch on ahead of you. Do you have the courage to do this?

Empathy—The Other Person's Moccasins

Here is a fascinating word—a fascinating topic, and an extremely important thing to master. I'm not really sure whether a person is born to some extent with it or whether this is totally given to him by the environment in which he finds himself and which he helps to create. But empathy is defined as "the imaginative projection of one's personality into that of another person." To put it less technically it simply means the ability to put yourself in the other person's shoes.

It is essential to be able to do this before you can practice the Golden Rule and attain the serenity, the feeling of accomplishment and peace of mind that follows.

Empathy is absolutely essential to selling your ideas, it is essential to inspiring others, to communicating with others, to sensing the correct social acts to perform, it's essential to knowing the correct type of courtesy to use in a given occasion. Empathy is absolutely essential to the truly accomplished and, in the most wholesome sense of the word, sophisticated person. To achieve empathy there is no single step that guarantees achievement. It is a blending of all of the major ideas advanced here. It does of course require that you *get out of yourself*. It does of course require that you develop, not merely lip service, but a real down-to-earth genuine interest in others. Until you *listen* with mind, heart and soul you cannot develop empathy. As long as you use words like empathy glibly and do not approach the acquisition of this with some humility you will probably never master this very vital *instrument* or *technique* or *gift* of effective human relations.

Application of Human Understanding

We could perhaps elaborate on this particular title by saying application of human understanding is through application of human underpinning, because the underpinning of human nature is just as important as the underpinning, undergirding, or footings of the modern skyscraper. You can no more cultivate a true understanding of motivation and a true understanding of meaningful and powerful human relations by simply learning when to smile, when to nod one's head, when to say "yes sir," when to say "no thank you ma'am," when to open a door, than you can fly!! These will simply make your behavior "acceptable, bland and a bit innocuous." At a given point in time, to truly understand the mainstream that sweeps people along toward their ultimate destiny of triumph or failure or some mediocre place in between, we must continue to focus (as we are throughout this book) upon basic values; upon basic beliefs because the quality of mind which we call tough-mindedness, the quality of mind which generates the motive power for the entire body, which makes it smile, which makes it say "yes ma'am," "no sir," "thank you," "by-your-leave sir"—these all come from a quality of mind, and the mind is made up of values, and the values are made up of beliefs—beliefs in the uniqueness, the dignity, and the essential goodness of people. These will come normally and naturally out of a deep understanding of what human beings fundamentally are, what they want, what they need, what creates in them destructive emotions, positive emotions and constructive emotions.

Basic Needs and Personal Goals

All people have four basic needs. These are *security, opportunity, recognition* and a *feeling of belonging*. It's important to understand these words in a bit more detail in order to understand what success really is. If you construe success to mean only a lot of money and a lot of material possessions, you will miss the total meaning here of basic needs, because at the most 20 per cent of security is concerned with financial security. I have seen and you have seen many people who have plenty of money, but who are among some of the most insecure people in the world because their basic needs are not being fulfilled for a feeling of significance, a feeling of being part of something that takes them out of themselves, a feeling of being recognized as human beings with basic dignity and a unique soul, who do not feel a part of a great adventure—the adventure called living. To feel that you understand people and that you have given them something, that you helped to weld together their basic needs and personal goals without a careful consideration of this particular kind of thing is to deal in *sophistry* which is defined as "sophistical or deceptively subtle reasoning or argumentation."

Building on Strengths
—Not Focusing on Weaknesses

When the book *Tough-Minded Management* was first written it became apparent how difficult it was going to be to adequately explain this idea because one of our most capable clients (a man who had built a large and successful business enterprise and with whom we had worked for some twenty-four months) read the manuscript and had a tendency to assume that this phrase "building on strengths—not focusing on weaknesses" meant to ignore the weaknesses of others, to overlook them—permissiveness. It is important for each reader to understand that this is *not* what we mean. When you set out to point out to somebody else how their performance can be improved (whether it be your child, your spouse, your boss, or your subordinates) it is important that the other person know that you are aware of the weakness, but when this has been done then *forget it*. You will gain nothing except to compress them, to paralyze them, to squeeze them down into insignificance by focusing on it and help make them feel that you will not forget it. You label yourself simply as a vindictive watchdog. So the better part of wisdom, the true course of wisdom here, is to concentrate on the strengths and accomplishments that this person possesses and to nurture, build, give direction and "how-to" with regard to these particular strengths.

Listening—The Essential Talent

Now as many of you know who have read the "Tough-Minded" books, a law called "Batten's Law of Communication" stresses that when a person does not achieve communication with another person he must assume that it was his fault until he has refined his communication, supplied the "why," and is assured that the other person understands fully what was intended. It is important in this connection that we do not use this *as an excuse for failure to listen.* Listening is absolutely vital.

I would like to talk to you a little bit about what is called Positive Listening. Too often we listen, on the premise that we've got something more worthwhile to say than the other person, thus we are in a hurry for him to finish his sentence so we can quickly say what we intended to say all the time. If you want to take the life and warmth and spontaneity out of a friendship, out of any relationship, just start negative listening—which means purely— that you hear the other person out only because the two of you can't talk at the same time and you reply with what you were going to say before he ever said anything. It doesn't take very much of this—fifteen or twenty minutes—before this person labels you consciously or subconsciously as a self-centered, arrogant ass. On the other hand, if you work hard at cultivating positive listening—and it does require hard work—if you listen to the other person with your whole attention he will know this and, interestingly enough, you will still know what to say when he is through talking and more important what you say will have much more meaning and much more power than what you would have said if you had carefully rehearsed it and waited only for him to complete his thought. Communication, not mere talking, is the "name of the game"—so, *listen!!* Perhaps the best technique of conversation is the ability to ask meaningful, interested questions and then listen with all pores open.

Hate Is a Mask for Fear

How about that? Isn't this a provocative statement? Hate is a mask for fear! It may be startling to some of you but this is absolutely true. When you see the individual who passes himself off as a strong and rugged man who feels that it is very important to project an aura of fearlessness—who engages in many destructive and vitriolic comments on all levels of government, on his competitor, on his boss, on minority groups, on all aspects of living he is simply putting up a trembling and tragic mask for the fear that he feels. On the other hand, the person who knows he has ability, who knows he has strengths, who has achieved some or many things, who has met some trials, tribulations and challenges and who has overcome them does not find it necessary to hate because he is not in fear of these minority groups, these associates, these so-called friends, competitors, etc. He is able to *give,* he is able to *rise above* petty considerations and he can look with a clear-eyed level gaze at such a hate-monger and say to himself "I feel sorry for that man, his feelings are motivated by fear, I am going to enlighten him and straighten him out, and if I can't get this done then I'm going to pay no attention to him."

Steps for Accomplishment

1. Put yourself in the other person's shoes. Learn to use empathy.
   A. Ask questions.
   B. Find out about his personal interests.
   C. Learn about his environment—his work, etc.
2. Accept the fact that each person is the center of their world and treat them accordingly.
3. Don't focus on weaknesses—size up the other person by determining his strengths.
4. Learn to love—in the true biblical sense—mankind.
5. Determine basic needs and personal goals of those you are trying to understand. Probe for these.
6. Scrape off the veneer! Look inside.
7. Listen—positively, and catalogue what you hear.
8. Forget your prejudices and biases—they will handicap you completely.
9. Don't let the "sophisticate" fool you.

10. Show sincere and genuine interest in the other person. Be courteous and gracious.

11. *Ask*—How will my attitude and action affect him? What should I do?

12. Above all—master the greatest laws and keys to human behavior ever written—the Sermon on the Mount.

Mere words are cheap and plenty enough, but ideas that rouse and set multitudes thinking come as gold from the mines.

A. OWEN PENNY

8

The Benefits to Them

The only way to achieve real motivation on the part of others with whom you work is to help them to see the *benefit to them* of doing what you want them to do.

TO BE UNDERSTOOD

Let's take a look now at the meaning of the word motivation. Motivation, broken down, simply means motive action or action to achieve motive. Thus the only way that you can help others to become motivated is to, first, understand what their motives are, and second, help them develop a pattern of action that they know will achieve their motives and help them above all to see *why*. So forget some of the tools and gimmicks that you have been taught to use in order to "motivate people." *You can't motivate anybody!!! I* can't motivate anybody. The only person who can bring about motivation is the individual himself. I cannot motivate you, I can only help you to define your own motive, to realize it, to strive toward it and to develop a pattern of action to get there. You might say that this entire book is one great big series of motivational sessions. We have worked with you from the very start to help you determine what your motives are. More importantly, to help you determine what your motives should be and can be, and the entire book is devoted squarely to helping you develop patterns of action, specific steps, specific "doing" things to achieve those motives. But you are the only one who can do this. This, in the final analysis, is all that motivation means.

Your Point—Pointed or Pointless

When you participate in a conversation, are you pointing the use of your words toward the accomplishment of some particular thing? Or are you talking in a meaningless circle simply to hear yourself and to enjoy the comforting realization that you are part of a conversation? If you converse for the latter reason I think it's just as well to realize right now that you are not really in a conversation, because when you talk simply to hear yourself talk, other people *seldom ever listen to you*. Unless you have in your own mind some particular point, some particular conversational objective, some particular thing that you are going to give in order to enlighten or to *point out*, then your conversation will very likely be pointless and you had better hold your tongue while you listen positively to the other person and develop a point of view that will be worthwhile conversing about.

A 19 year old laborer, a participant in one of the Successful Living Institute Success Planning Centers, asked the question, "What are the two basic factors of a conversation?" His classmates who were from the professions and executive positions and were considered to be more mature gave him many sophisticated answers. However, the answer he had in mind which was simple and basic was only "to understand and be understood." So often we try to sophisticate the simple and thus develop the image of complicated ignorant asses.

How to Sell—Or Kill—With Words

This is a really stimulating and challenging phrase, isn't it? We can sell our ideas, our enthusiasm, our attitudes, our values, our practices, our philosophy, so that other people see the benefit to them, so that they know what to do about it, so that they see their role in it, so that they are committed, so that they are involved, so that they see *why* and develop an understanding of their motives and the action required to achieve it—thus total motivation. This is real selling!!! Or, on the other hand, we can use the same amount of conversation with the same people and exercise the same amount of physical and mental energy, and we can dull and deaden the expressions that light the sparkle in the eye, the enthusiasm, the verve and the dash of other people with whom we talk. We can do this by failing to show them what they will gain by participating with them. We can expect them to become committed to our particular goal without appropriate involvement. We can withhold the "why" and say "That's my business," "You just do as I say and don't ask why." We can use tepid words, morbid words, negative words, dull words, blunt, pointless words. We can literally drain the enthusiasm and the life out of either a conversation or an entire party. For instance, it is realistic to recognize that a number of people have some negative emotions in them. If you are one of these people, and by now I'm sure you recognize what negative thinking is—defeatist, self-oriented, self-centered thinking—then let me give you this little challenge with both some facetiousness and some seriousness. *Go completely negative.* Say that you expect the bomb to fall any day. You are against free enterprise, you are against democracy—you are for Communism—you're against health, you're for sickness—you're against personal integration, you are for personal fragmentation—you are against accomplishment, you are for failure—in short, you are a totally sick, negative, self-preoccupied, messy personality, and if you think enough of this kind of thing *then make it your creed!* Say, "I am opposed to everything, I believe in nothing except failure," and shout this as being your creed, and *if you don't think enough of it to make it your creed, then why even mess with it?*

Think Big But Speak Simply

Another secret of men like Churchill was that the size of the words they used were small. They spoke in a language that could be understood by the untutored, the illiterate, the masses of the world. They were able to speak simply because they thought big, because they had so thoroughly filled their word arsenal with words and word combinations and an understanding of words that they were then able to pick the right combination. For instance, a man such as Churchill and a man such as Franklin D. Roosevelt were able to pick the one best word that could be understood, simply because they, in most instances, knew at least three synonyms for that word, and usually these synonyms were much bigger. So the person who truly knows how to communicate is a person who has made a study of words to the point where, automatically running through his mind are three or four alternatives for every big word and he is able to come up with the simplest one and fit it together smoothly so that it flows and creates a total impact. So *learn* lots of big words and then *use* as many small ones as you logically can.

Action Words and Concepts

Here are three key considerations in the skillful use of action words and concepts which reflect that you think big, but that you can communicate simply.

1) The skillful use of words does more harm than good unless you *believe* in, *feel* and *are* what you say.

2) A contrived or insincere interest in the other person rarely yields the best results. Such insincerity is usually sensed even when it is not consciously realized.
3) There are words which make the other person feel a quickening of the pulse. All relatively normal people want to live long and they want to be healthy. So try words which are morbid, turbid, sordid, sickly, silly or moribund and note both the conscious and unconscious pulling away which results. On the other hand, watch the reaction to words which smack of growth, zest, pep, sprightliness, expansion, health and sparkle. It should go without saying, however, that the results you get, while better, will be limited if you use even the best chosen words for their sake alone. Rather, make people feel a sense of stretch and growth in direct response to the dynamically conceived words you use and *feel*. We mentioned a little earlier the business of how to sell or kill with words. Let me give you some real stumbling blocks to selling with words; some real fine ways to kill with words. Here is the way to take some enthusiasm and meaning right out of any kind of living situation. (1) "Let's get back to reality." (2) "You're way ahead of your time." (3) "You can't teach an old dog new tricks." (4) "The public would never go for it." (5) "It's against our policy." (6) "Let's table it for now." (7) "Has anyone else tried it?" (8) "We'll be a laughing stock." (9) "We've never done it before." (10) "That's not our problem." The toughminded individual, the truly positive person faces up squarely to this kind of objection. He stresses simple, direct words in setting forth required end results and insists upon real accomplishment.

Communication by Osmosis

In recent years, the word "communication" has been used, probably not thousands, but millions of times and very seldom used in its full and real sense. Communication has been largely interpreted to mean the transmitting of information through either spoken or written words. This is just a very small, and, in some instances, an insignificant part in the total process of communication:

Hal Batten has developed a concept he calls "Communication By Osmosis." This has to do with the type of communication which takes place through facial expression, through tone of voice, through posture, through every physical and emotional shred of energy which is transmitted either for the person to whom you are communicating and for what you hope to communicate—or it is dragging back, holding onto and impeding total communication. The thing that you are *against* keeps leaking and seeping in insidiously and coloring your communication with negative overtones so that the person to whom you wish to communicate either feels defensive, confused, resentful, diffident, or in some particular way does not feel motivated to enthusiastically grasp the full meaning of what you are attempting to communicate, grasping this with the full intention of doing something vigorous and worthwhile about it. "What you *are* speaks so loudly, I can't hear what you're *saying*." So see this challenge as one which looks you squarely in the eye. If you are not communicating to people in your neighborhood, in your city, in your job, this is not their fault; it's your fault. And, *whenever you point one finger at another individual, three fingers are pointing back at you.* So, analyze not only your words for simplicity and clarity, but also look below the surface and analyze yourself and your very posture, your very tone of voice, for sincerity of purpose and desire to actually accomplish something in the process of communicating.

Steps for Accomplishment

1. Show the benefit to *them!*
2. Make your points—pointed not pointless.
3. For the rest of your life continue to learn new words and use them appropriately.

4. Use emotion-generating words—which build on strengths.

5. Remember that words alone is not communication. Review communication by osmosis on page 107.

6. Study Batten's Law of Communication. "When the communicatee does not understand exactly what the communicator intended, the responsibility remains that of the communicator."

7. Remember your objective—"to be understood."

8. Organize your presentation—whether it is to a group of one or one thousand.

9. The best time to prepare an oral presentation is right after you have heard one.

You will never be the person you can be if pressure, tension and discipline are taken out of your life.
                    DR. JAMES G. BILKEY

9 Live, Love and Laugh

MAKE TENSION AN ASSET–THE MUSIC OF TAUT STRINGS

It can be very damaging and naive to try to overlook the fact that we have emotions, to try and bury them and maintain an aloof, glacial and bland exterior to the entire world. Back in the early 'fifties certain studies came out which seemed to show a strong relationship between degenerative, nervous diseases and responsible executive and professional jobs. I recall in particular one man who said "I'll never be caught by tension, I'm going to stay unruffled, I will not let anybody create any tension in me, I will surround myself by an environment that is calm and unruffled." About three months after this statement this man *had developed a nice ulcer!* He was locking tensions up in himself. He was not letting the normal flow of emotions express themselves and escape him. He was building up internally a hot, broiling, writhing furnace of emotions and the tissues inside his vital organs suffered because of this. Something had to give. So this man had made of tension a very negative and destructive thing. Subsequently he was told that if he continued to build up these tensions and lock them in and offer this bland controlled face at all times to the world he would certainly shorten his life. He was urged to Live, Love and Laugh. He was counseled on the fact that there are two kinds of tension in life. Tension is essential and very important to the good life. The Almighty never intended for a man to live the life of a vegetable without surging, racing emotions and emotions cause a tenseness of tissue, a tenseness of mind and brain, thus the actual meaning of the word tense is tension. But as I say, there are two kinds.

Let me illustrate this by describing the amateur and the pro. The amateur speaker, for instance, may very well have delivered 50 or 60 speeches and still be an amateur. What makes him an amateur? When he stands up in the group he has a tendency to think about himself, to wonder what the audience is thinking of him. He wonders if he is properly groomed, he wonders if his hair is unmussed, he wonders if he looks alert and intelligent that day. He wonders if people are going to snicker at him, he wonders if they are going to be bored, he wonders if they are going to be hostile. His emotions are *coming in on him* and they can literally consume him, tighten him up, cause heart attacks, cause nervous breakdowns and all of the related degenerative diseases. On the other hand, the professional speaker can be a professional after only 8 or 10 speeches if he visualizes his role in front of the audience as being to give them something to use to make their life better, to make them more efficient, to make their entire existence more meaningful. Thus he sees that his only justification for taking up the time of a group of people is to *give* them something. If he is up there simply to get, the pleasure of having plodded through a presentation so that he can chalk this up as another professional or business credit, that's all it will amount to. And it will be a hollow attention-producing effort indeed, because the true pro gets up in front of the group and he probably has even more tension than the amateur, but this tension is flowing out from him and reaching out and enveloping, affecting, and energizing his audience.

Speakers are only an example. This applies in every phase of living. The wife who decides that she will endure every little indignity that a gross or boorish husband may inflict on her and the family will build up a nice batch of tension internally and develop a lot of complications. On the other hand she may express these tensions in various ways, by scrubbing the floor extra hard, by working extra hard and perhaps this will help her. The man who decides that he will bottle up every source of tension that his wife creates ultimately reaches a point where he is liable to desert the family, drop dead, or haul off and slap his wife. There is no substitute for letting the emotions come out and be directed in terms of constructive action, wholesome physical exercise, and meaningful or even inconsequential talking. The secret—to a great extent—in minimizing destructive tensions in effective family life is to "talk it out." These are three simple little words but they hold a very powerful key to draining off destructive tensions and turning them into constructive conversation, enlightenment and serenity.

Tension—Motivating or Killing

We have said that tension can be very productive, that it can be positive, that it can be good. And this is particularly true when each individual knows the motives that will guide his life from here on. Then he has a goal to point toward; he has a direction in which to fuse and focus his energy. We have from time to time used the expression "the shortest distance between two points is a straight line." This is equally true in making constructive use of tension. When we have purpose to our days, purpose for our weekends, purpose in a job and in the course and direction of our family living, then we can let loose great amounts of outgoing, ebullient tension and make this achieve some very worthwhile things. If we decide to lock it up within us we must be aware of the fact that we are virtually sentencing ourselves to ill health and to certain negative and destructive reactions. This is not to rule out the value and essential nature of self-discipline, but again we have to look here at the nature of self-discipline. It has been defined as self-training which strengthens, molds and develops. So, if we pour our tensions into action patterns, into words, into expressions, into daily habits which build, strengthen and develop, we need have no fear of tension as an enemy; but on the other hand, we can readily recognize it and feel good about it as a true asset.

Fear—Foundation for Disaster

Perhaps the greatest single source of unhappiness in the world today is *fear*, a nameless, seemingly groundless thing called fear. Fear is a fog hovering over the world soaking in and dampening us as we move through life, and it is all so unnecessary. This is not to say that fear is easily eradicated, but there are definite principles and guideposts which will point the way if people will only apply them. To discuss toughminded performance in this competitive world without treating fear would be to dodge a vital issue. Fears can multiply rapidly if we let them, but fears are destructive largely because of the ignorance of the people involved, and this statement in no way excludes highly educated people. Vast numbers of people have not had the opportunity to discover what can be done in a truly productive climate to eradicate fear.

People develop fears for a number of reasons. Among the stumbling blocks to letting oneself go and ridding oneself of fear is fear of failure, of superiors and subordinates, fear of pressure, fear of being labeled as timid, fear of failure thus becoming a perfectionist—habits which are repetitive and which compound vast negative patterns and attitudes which are based only on the past and the status quo. The answer to the eradication of fear, again, is so simple that one is apt to dismiss it cynically and say "I tried it and it didn't work." But for the person who has discipline and determination, a complete, thorough and profound reading of the New Testament will provide much enlightenment and do much to eradicate fear. Then turn around and read it again and again—tieing in every truth there with the other truths and the specific techniques you have been learning in this book. Bit by bit you begin to wash away the legacy of fear that you may have built up in your childhood. You may have been told a number of things which your parents genuinely believed, but which are no longer applicable. Concepts which propound fear of God instead of love of God, which teach a sad grim approach to Christianity rather than an enlightened optimistic buoyant approach. The only way you can clear this up in your own mind is to make a thorough study of this greatest of all sources of basic truths.

Jacques Maritain, the Christian Existentialist, has said:

> When he (man) obeys the law as a friend of the law because the Spirit of God renders him one in spirit and love with the principle of the law, and does of his own accord that which the law commands, he is no longer under the law; it is his own love, now sovereign and sovereignly free, his love of his God and his All, which causes him to obey the law that has now become his law, the personal call by which the word of Him he loves reaches him. This is a law in regard to which he is no longer a *self* to be identified with *everyman*. He is *this man* himself, this man answering to his own name, to whom the law speaks in his pure solitude with God.[1]

Here he is saying (existentially) that man's love of God *can* enable him to transcend fear by giving much of himself to others if the true definition of God is, "God is Love."

It is also very important to recognize that many of the people who generate in us certain fearful reactions are people who desire our compassion and our help much more than our fear. Until we look behind the behavior of the domineering boss, the blusterer,

---

[1] *Existence and the Existent*, Jacques Maritain, copyright 1948, Pantheon Books, Inc. Reprinted by permission of Random House, Inc.

the bully, the master of the perfect squelch (and recognize that this is almost always motivated by *fear* on his part) until we do this we can do very little to eradicate our own fear of him. So let's recognize that all anti-social behavior is prompted primarily by fear on the part of the individual who manifests it, and recognize that we have a worthwhile challenge in front of us to help this man get over his fears, to shift from negative to positive, to shift from what he is *against* to what he is *for,* and in the very process we very clearly begin to shape up an attitude and a daily pattern of courage which renders fear a very negligible roadblock to our future success. "Life is too short to waste precious moments in fear of nothing."

Are They Really Out to Get You?

Doesn't that sound ominous? Are they really out to get you? We have of course a particular kind of psychosis called paranoia where the individual has the deep-seated feeling that others are out to persecute him. This can only be treated adequately by a trained professional psychiatrist. It is well for the relatively normal, relatively well-adjusted person however to recognize that you're not really that important. *Nobody's really out to get you.* You can build this up in your mind to a point where it truly becomes a ghost, where it truly becomes a persecuting straw man.

For instance, let's take a look at the shy person. If you have a tendency to withdraw from certain social situations, if you have a tendency to withdraw from a confrontation with your boss, if you have a tendency to avoid (through a series of well contrived excuses) certain social engagements, in short—all kinds of affairs that take you into active contact with a lot of people and you say with an apologetic and sometimes rather proud smile, "I guess I'm just shy, I'm bashful, always have been and guess I always will be," my temptation would be to say to you privately but with considerable sincerity and feeling, "What makes you think you're that important? *Who do you think you are?* How conceited can you get?" Because, you see, the basis of shyness, the basis of so-called bashfulness is almost always an exaggerated feeling that others are going to be looking at you, analyzing you, out to get you, being concerned with you, ready to focus on your weaknesses, and the bald fact is *it just ain't so*. People don't care that much about you!!

The only way people really care enough about you to give you a lot of attention is when you have shown a real interest in them, when you learn to listen to them with interest, with sincerity, when you learn to ask penetrating questions, when you have indicated that you have some interest in *giving* them something. This will build a real interest in you on their part, but certainly the usual passive withdrawal type of thing which we call shyness and bashfulness is usually simply a comfortable set of crutches to enable you to wallow in your self-preoccupation without getting too unhappy because *nobody's out to get you*. The only person who can get you is *you!!*

The Business of Living a Long Time

Walter Pitkin has this to say in his book *Life Begins at Forty* (Simon and Schuster): "If life begins at forty, then most of us have only fifteen or sixteen years to live." This was hurled at me by one sincere dispenser of gloom, who went on to cite (with deadly accuracy) statistics showing that most Americans die in their mid-fifties.

A bitter thought, isn't it? But I think most physicians and psychologists will agree with me that *Americans die young largely because they never start living*. Our silly dollar-chasing and our greasy grind of factory and our stupid philosophies of life all carry over into the middle years the tempo and thrust of youth. The regular trick of the big business organization is to fill young men with rosy dreams of swift promotion and wealth; to drive them to the limit as junior executives or as foremen; and then to trust to dull human nature to hold the pace as a matter of habit.

After thirty-seven, Americans die off fast. Their kidneys, hearts, and blood vessels give way, as a rule. By fifty-five, the death rate is shocking. If, having abused themselves until their fortieth birthdays, they are seized with the typical panic of oncoming middle age and try to begin living, they may succeed; but they will probably pass from the scene in their late fifties; for the deeper damage to body and spirit has been done.

If you wish to begin living after forty and to keep on living until threescore and ten, you must start planning at ten. This is a platitude of such green antiquity that I am ashamed to echo it here; but it must enter our records. Start right, and forty will be high noon. You could live to be eighty, hale and hearty—barring accidents and bad ancestors.

How about this for a challenge? The Mayo Clinic after years of deep research states that the best life must consist of four balanced parts: Work, Love, Play and Worship. Destroy this balance and you invite disease, worry and decay.

In recent years a number of studies have been made of the kind of people we often refer to affectionately as the "sprightly oldster." The man or woman who is in his 80's and and 90's, sometimes past 100, who seems to be spare and spry and bright-eyed, who seems to spread some good will and good feeling wherever he goes, is of course always plagued with the question "What do you think is your great secret?" Well, of course, many of these people have looked back with a twinkle in their eye and said "Because I smoke 14 cigars a day or because I never had a sober day in my life" or some such thing, and many times don't give you a definite answer—here lies one of the keys. These people have learned to develop a resilient, buoyant, humorous reaction to life, and this is one of the basic secrets.

The sound sociological, anthropological and psychiatric research that has been conducted has, however, isolated three principal things. They are: they learned fairly early in life to work, that much involvement in work, commitment to work, can be fun, can be pleasant, can be every bit as pleasant if not more so, than play itself. They never quit learning. Never!! They continue to read, they continue to ask questions, they continue to want to travel, they continue to query about the "why" of the world around them, the society around them, the culture around them. They are outgoing individuals. They do not regard young people as their enemies but rather as their greatest sources of delight. And last but certainly not least, they learned to make tension an asset by turning it into humor. A loud and genuine belly-laugh is a form of tension, but it is a form of very helpful, healthful, replenishing, and constructive tension. So here are some simply stated, but key building blocks in the foundation of a long and happy life. In summary: they loved to work, stayed mentally curious, and had a sense of humor. *They lived passionately!*

A very important and pervasive source of peace of mind under pressure is to build deep into your consciousness a fundamental and deep understanding of what is *right;* how you react to people in quandaries, how you react to others. It is particularly vital here to understand that many people who seem to be deliberately offensive to you are people who are this way in *spite* of themselves not *because* of themselves. The average individual in our world today wants very much to be a fine individual, a good person, well-adjusted, happy, healthy. The fact that they may act in quite a variety of ways and do not seem happy, cheerful, helpful or healthy (*and you must carve this indelibly in your mind*), is simply that they are this way *in spite of themselves* and *not because of themselves.* Once you thoroughly understand this, your tolerance, your flexibility, your ability to rise above pettiness, above smallness, is greatly aided, and you are then able to retain peace of mind in many a tense and pressure filled situation when otherwise you would succumb to the same weak emotions that they do and play right into their hands in an amateur-like way instead of being a real pro who uses his emotions in a positive way, who reaches out *to understand, to build* and *to aid* the other person. This may seem from time to time a bit of a "sweetness and light" type of thing, but it requires individuals with a much greater amount of real manhood, real womanhood, real strength, real toughness than the cynic who reacts with angry, weak and negative emotionalism.

In order to master fear, eliminate it, and make it bow to its master (which is self-confidence); to blast anxiety, eliminate bashfulness and shyness; to become in short a whole person, a vibrant person with faith in self, in man, and in the world around you—it is particularly important to understand the defense mechanisms which make many people act as they do. As we have said earlier, nobody wants to be a "so-and'so"; they are this way *in spite of themselves* and *not because of themselves*.

The Shift From Problems to Challenges

Shift your emphasis from problems to challenges. The relationship of this concept to tension is very close. When you have problems you worry about them. When you have challenges you are working, applying and attacking this plan to get results. The shift in thinking from problems to challenges is important in making tension an asset. Don't let your unsolved problems pursue you, make your decisions and forget them, and then do your job as well as you can.

The essential difference between the unhappy, neurotic type person and the happy, normal person is the difference between *get* and *give*. The unhappy person is concerned with: the world is against me, the town is against me, the family is against me, what's in it for me, what are people doing to me, and so forth. When your central theme in life is *getting* you usually do *get* headaches. But the happy person is looking toward what he can *do*, what he can *give*, what he can *accomplish*.

We have seen people who were born and raised in destitute surroundings. Most looked about them and decided life was loaded with *problems*. A few discovered some of the secrets of living and looked upon changing their circumstances as a series of challenges.

With the passing years there are countless examples of the relationship between productive work and a long life. I recall a man who had been retired two years, who had wasted away rapidly and who felt he had very little time left. He had looked forward to retirement eagerly and upon reaching 65 he literally turned himself off so he could "enjoy life." He found new inner tensions building. He smoked, ate and drank more and his blood pressure rose. And although he began to feel worse and worse, doctors could find nothing organically wrong. Various people suggested various hobbies. Since this has become an overworked word similar to "golden age" or "senior citizen," he rebelled and considered such activity insipid.

One day, by happenstance, a small child asked him to fix a broken toy. He couldn't turn the child down and painfully set about fixing the toy. Other children discovered he was vulnerable and began to ask him to do other similar work. He was amazed some weeks later when he realized he was looking forward eagerly to the next day—was finding time to smoke and have a drink only occasionally and beginning to savor his leisure time. While he didn't need the money, he put out a sign advertising his ability to do repair work and when last contacted at the age of 73, he said he had never felt better.

Accept Yourself

Real maturity of wisdom comes when an individual has learned to face honestly, himself, his times, his problems and their solutions based on things over which he has control—and still enjoy life.

Dr. Neibuhr's famous quotation, which in slightly different form is also the alcoholic's anonymous prayer, is apt to this discussion. It is as follows: "Give me the courage to change what can be changed, the serenity to accept that which can't, and the wisdom to know the difference."

1. Recognize that there are two types of problems, those that you can do something about and those over which you have no control.
2. Learn to live in your environment.

How to Deal with Tensions

In order to use positive tensions it is necessary to get rid of negative tensions. The National Association for Mental Health in their booklet "How to Deal with Your Tensions" list eleven things you can do.

1. Talk it out.
2. Escape for a while.
3. Work off your anger.
4. Give in occasionally.
5. Do something for others.
6. Take one thing at a time.
7. Shun the "Superman" urge.
8. Go easy with your criticism.
9. Give the other fellow a break.
10. Make yourself available.
11. Schedule your recreation.

Make Tension an Asset

Remember that tension can be valuable. This must be tension which bounces out of your mind and out of your body and is transmitted toward other people—which reaches out and *gives* them additional encouragement, warmth, guidance, direction and purpose. The kind of tensions which come in on you through preoccupation only with yourself, your imagined ills, your preoccupation with getting and with what you are against, can virtually eat out the lining of your stomach.

Remember that ministers, doctors, lawyers, live longer not because they do not work as hard or are exposed to as much tension, but because many of them develop *a feeling of mission which pulls them completely out of themselves.* They become truly concerned if they are true "pros" with giving more than they get. Thus, they *get* and *get* and *get*.

MAKE TENSION AN ASSET

Again, let us refer to the seven day test. If you want to make the next seven days sick, meaningless, full of self-preoccupation, gray and futile; concentrate only on what you can *get*. If you want to make the next seven days the most wonderful of your life, concentrate solely on what you can give and recognize that the most precious thing you can give is yourself.

Time and again when we have issued this challenge to people of varied occupational backgrounds, various kinds of dispositions, heights, weights, ages, to go all out—to devote every waking moment to reaching out and building other people, we have had these people come back in the weeks, the months and the years that followed and say, "I wonder why I didn't discover this myself. It's all so simple. I was looking somehow for a complex answer to happiness. Some kind of a devious system or set of mystical formulae where I could magically press a button and happiness would turn on and glow throughout me. Instead I have found that all it takes is to get up each morning deciding that I will give a little bit of myself to every person with whom I come in contact. This has made my life abundant and rich, both physically, mentally and financially, beyond my puny imagination of some time ago."

Certainly history has shown us that most truly great thoughts, words, and deeds are almost always preceded by obstacles, adversities and tragedies.

The key question is this—will you extract from these obstacles, the positives and grow because of them—or will you extract the negative and retreat and wither because of them?

Dr. Albert Schweitzer put it this way:

"I don't know what your destiny will be, but one thing I know: the only ones among you who will be really happy are those who will have sought and found how to serve."

Steps for Accomplishment

1. 1-11. Action Steps 1 through 11 are on page 122. These are to cope with negative tensions.

12. The following exercise is to develop tensions.

List in this column examples of when you feel tension or pressure (either positive or negative).	List here any negative reactions you currently have to any of the situations. Determine how you can avoid it.	Study and analyze each situation to determine how you can make tension in each case serve a positive purpose—then put it to work.
_____	_____	_____
_____	_____	_____
_____	_____	_____
_____	_____	_____
_____	_____	_____
_____	_____	_____
_____	_____	_____
_____	_____	_____

. . . Man has too long forgotten that the ultimate economic and spiritual unit of any civilization is still the family.

CLAIRE BOOTH LUCE

10 Unity and Faith

THE UNIFIED FAMILY

Perhaps the most important single institution in the world today is the family. And the family is being subjected to pressures, disrupting influences, forces of division, diffidence and degeneracy, to an extent probably never experienced before, or at least not since the days of Sodom and Gomorrah. The family holds the secret to the future of our way of life in this country. The family can steadily disintegrate and become a group of individuals who think purely of themselves, where fathers and mothers simply want to get the children raised so they can get them out of their hair and then "relax and feel secure."

The family can continue in many instances to simply be a sort of sexual gratification for husband and wife, a place for the children to eat, to refuel their bodies, to receive certain exhortations and/or chiding at best about their report cards, and then go on happily about their own individual ways. This can continue in many communities throughout the nation and the basic purpose of our Constitution can gradually fall completely apart until its unified fabric becomes a meaningless patchwork of tatters and rags. Or, on the other hand, the family can become a dynamic symbol of the power of unity and faith.

There are many fine families in the United States today and in almost every instance the truly happy family is where children can speak frankly to the mother and father and where mother and father feel a strong interest in the children. These families, without exception, are families in which a great amount of faith in God abounds. This is the family where the father has reached a point of tough-mindedness where he finds no occasion to lower his voice when he speaks of God, of Christ, or of any other deity of a deep religious faith. The same, of course, is equally true of the mother.

This kind of a family recognizes that a family starts off with a man and woman being united in a complete spirit of unity by the religious sacrament provided for by the Almighty Creator. Many families in the early years in the search for new pleasures, new furniture, a new home, a certain carving out of social status and of occupational security, realize this only in a fleeting way. Perhaps the average, or at least the majority, of young couples in the first ten years of their married life go to church erratically at best, and then note an increase. Regrettably, in many instances, this is still a thing to do because it's "good for the kids."

Recently Dr. Louis H. Valbracht, one of the great ministers of our time, participated in a question-and-answer session. The question was, "What is the one best way to interest young children, children of all ages, in church attendance and participation? What is the one best way to help give them, at their early informative age, a dynamic, meaningful understanding of the value of an active church life?" He answered promptly, "Parents who set them a real church-going example." The growing, maturing boy's conception of what a real man is, is conditioned, probably 80% or 90%, by the kind of man his father is. The boy who is going to grow up and be all man, think tall and participate in the community life of his country as a fine and worthwhile citizen has two strikes against him if his father is anything less. The girl who is going to grow up to maturity, to adulthood, and be a fine, gentle, dedicated inspirational mother and wife has, by the same token, two strikes against her if her mother is anything less.

Recently, while delivering a speech to the American Salesmasters Congress in Kansas City, I heard a gentleman receive his award as one of the greatest salesmen for the 1965. He was a handsome, assured, and fine looking man, and while there he was asked "How do you help your son to want to be a real salesman." His answer was a thoughtful one. He said, "They say a picture is better than a thousand words. There's one thing even better than a picture. The best possible image is a person. So, if you want to help your son, don't just use words, don't place in front of him just a picture, place in front of him a *man*."

Emotions That Destroy and Decay

Perhaps the greatest contribution to the destruction and division of a family is the feeling on the part of any one member that they are not truly wanted. When a child feels unwanted he begins to lapse into certain negative and antisocial behavior. He throws tantrums, he may feign, or actually feel illness, he may become accident prone, he may do any number of things which subconsciously get him the attention that is being denied him by thoughtless or maladjusted parents. The same thing is true on the parental level. If the husband feels rejected by his wife he can become increasingly demonstrative in a negative way. He points out to her boisterously what kind of a man he is, how big and powerful he is, how he told "that old s.o.b." that he works for where to go, he tells her about how he is going to get the knife in his competitor before the competitor can slip it in him. He tells her slyly about how he is cheating on his income tax. He may let it slip out subtly that he is still pretty attractive to other women and is having a difficult time to keep from succumbing to them, in the misleading notion that this will create in his wife a greater interest in him.

Emotions That Build and Enrich

Is there anything more wonderful than being a man? Is there anything more wonderful than being a woman? I think it is absolutely essential that every man realize that to a woman there is nothing more wonderful than being truly feminine, that every woman should realize that to a man there is nothing more wonderful than being truly masculine. Perhaps the failure to recognize this many times detracts from emotions that build and enrich. Many men have the mistaken notion that true masculinity is so great that perhaps women want to be masculine instead of feminine, because femininity, they may feel, is in some way second-rate. Thus they treat their wives in a somewhat masculine manner and then wonder why they do not have the cheerful, willing lover which they seek; thus their own male vanity becomes damaged and they begin to strike back, indulge in sarcasm, indulge in innuendoes about how alluring they are to other women and the whole process of emotions that destroy and decay are set into motion.

So it's vital that first of all each partner realize that the other one must be made to feel fully and vibrantly a member of their particular gender. Time and again we know of women who, taut and wan of face, ask the question, "What do people want from me? What am I supposed to be?" We pick up magazines, and we see such articles as "What it is to be a woman," or "What is wrong with women today," or "How to make him feel more important," or "Are you neglecting your job," etc., etc., without very much variation.

Whenever you settle for a complex solution to any problem you settle for second best. With few exceptions—if any—the most simple, direct and truthful approach to the solution of a problem is the best. Let me recommend then, first of all to the wife, that she take this direct, simple approach to creating a marriage which constantly builds and enriches. I recommend to each woman that she create an opportunity to talk with her husband, free from any type of interruption, and ask him sincerely and directly to think deeply, and tell her exactly *what kind of woman he wants her to be*. What kind of wife, what kind of mother, what kind of friend, what kind of lover, and if the occasion has been carefully enough set, and if he is given time to think deeply about this and tell her, here is one of the most solid, rockribbed bases for the future of a marriage that one could possibly conceive.

At the same time I recommend that the husband do precisely the same thing. Plan the occasion carefully, give her time to think, make clear that this request comes from the heart, that it is absolutely genuine and motivated by love—and then find out in some detail precisely what she feels her husband, father, friend and lover should be. Again, he has a master blueprint that can only be improved by saturating the action steps each day, each month, all of the coming years with love and a deep and abiding faith. Because, if you lack a deep and meaningful faith in God, you cannot fully trust yourself—hence, others cannot fully trust you. How *practical* can you get? There is *nothing* more practical than such a deep and practicing faith.

In addition to laying these blocks of granite for the foundation of a healthy and harmonious family life we find that the often-repeated but never trite phrase "the family that prays together stays together" cannot be improved upon. This is so vital. Time and again we have seen families who hesitantly gave this a try and who testify later on with glowing eyes and vibrant soul that they will never again let a division or fissure enter into the perfect unity, the one pure and towering peak called the family.

To avoid the tragic trap which is all too often waiting for the unwary, we must avoid any action which makes a woman feel less feminine in her marriage, and any action which makes a man feel less masculine.

Now there is unfortunately a lot of hogwash which suggests that a woman must at all times submerge her own identity and her own desires and always be waiting for her husband with cheerful and sugary statements which make him feel like a big hero at the end of each day. This flies in the face of common sense and practicality. There are days when she is going to be tired. There are days when he does not require this kind of thing when he comes home. There is no set and rigid routine by any stretch of the imagination that a husband or wife can go through to create unified family life. There are simply a set of fundamental truths which can from time to time be applied to a series of steps. These fundamental truths of course are the privilege of sharing a common spiritual knowledge and gratification, the need to have had their marriage initially sanctified in a church, and the need to recognize that family life *is not two people,* but that in the eyes of God a family *is one,* that any outside influences that may interrupt the essential unity of this family must be rigorously cast out.

The art of positive listening is perhaps more important in avoiding the tragic traps of marriage than any other particular technique that can be recommended. The best is always the most simple. The complex solution to any kind of problem is always second best. Thus the best advice is the simple little three word sentence "Talk it out." This is more challenging and more important than it may seem. There are times when it is so comfortable to hide behind a facade of hurt feelings and sullenness and to sulk a while. All this does is distress and befuddle, perhaps even anger, the partner, and causes in yourself nothing but a withdrawal. Karl Menninger has said that passivity is the greatest weakness of the inadequate husband and father.

There is an important distinction here between talking a thing over and talking it out. Talking a thing over can many times make the subject tiresome and repetitious. Talking it out means to discuss the particular challenge until agreement is reached on what should be done about it, and then *avoid needless repetition.*

The Rocky Road

A major roadblock to the free and unimpeded enjoyment of the highway of marriage is the difficulty of admitting our inadequacies, or our weaknesses or our mistakes to each other as marriage partners. In the early years of a marriage this can sometimes be easier than the middle years because as the personality many times congeals (as a person begins to play what they feel is the desired role in the eyes of their spouse) they begin to build certain static, rigid concepts of themselves. If the man has felt it necessary to build in his wife's eyes the image of the hero that never makes a mistake he is going to find as the years go by that it is very difficult to admit to his wife that he has made a mistake. But if he's tough-minded, if he's determined to have a successful family life he's got to recognize that as sure as he lives she's going to see those mistakes anyway and his failure to admit them frankly and openly stamps him increasingly as a small man and builds an increasingly invisible, but very real wall between them.

Face up to oneself and say "I guess I exploded when I shouldn't have, it's my fault" and even though sometimes you may feel it's about 50-50, if you can say this and feel it and look at your wife with a smile and say "It was my fault," you're going to find that the occasions for saying this become less and less. Perhaps of even greater importance is the ability to graciously and warmly accept an apology and be able to say to your mate, "Certainly I had some share in this and let's simply resolve we won't let it happen again." Let the warmth flow, let the smile flash, let the eyes sparkle, and above all let forgiveness and compassion rule.

Here's a real challenge to the tough-minded woman, to the tough-minded man. Do you have the courage to refrain from projecting the blame for every little thing that goes wrong on that of your spouse? Do you have the courage to rigorously review your own behavior, to recognize that whenever you point a finger, three fingers are pointing back at you. This is the kind of challenge that you've got to take all of your married life. So recognize it rigorously, review your own role, your own part in whatever goes wrong, and cheerfully and freely take at least your share of blame for it (perhaps a little more) and you will find less and less reason to have to apologize and to accept blame as the years go by, because the path of the good marriage founded upon compassion, founded upon mutual love, founded upon tough-minded positivism, goes increasingly smooth.

The Warm and Wonderful Way

This might very well be subtitled "Sympathy, empathy, understanding, compassion, comfort, cooperation." Any number of fine words get at this business of achieving the warm and wonderful way of family life. But let's be sure and not kid ourselves. It cannot possibly be 100 per cent smooth and devoid of rocks all the way. The important thing is that each spouse sit down with husband or wife and review the principles of tough-minded living over and over again. Keeping an open mind, radiating compassion, praying together, talking it out, and then making sure that you uninhibitedly let the children see the practice of this particular way of living. We have concentrated primarily on the relationship between husband and wife. This has been deliberate because the children shape their philosophy on the example they see in front of them day after day. Normally the healthy, well-adjusted, happy family discovers a lot of normal, healthy, well-adjusted people in their own community because we usually have mirrored back to us that which we project. The erratic, persecuted, negative family will usually find themselves surrounded by a similar group.

Continue the process of self-analysis, continue the process of reviewing all the principles of tough-minded living. Invite your children to participate if they are old enough.

Grow Old Happily

The process of aging can be a grim, bitter and grudging fight against the encroachment of time. We can study our emerging wrinkles and our changing hair color bitterly. Or we can make of the total aging process a warm and wonderful and happy experience. The important thing is that we recognize what the objective at the end of the road may be. One of the best ways to insure that moving through life toward greater maturity and old age can be a mellow and pleasant experience, is to work together increasingly to convert everything that you are *against* to what you are *for*.

When a husband and wife sit down together and decide after each has developed a complete list of what he or she is *against* and a complete list of what he or she is *for*, they are going to cooperate very closely, are going to talk freely about the progress they are making in converting from hate to love, from suspicion to assurance, from cynicism to buoyancy, in short, completing the transfer fully of the negative attributes to the positive levels of living. There is no need to be lonely. There is no reason why any family in the United States cannot ultimately arrive at a successful marriage. It would be naive and pollyanna-ish indeed to say that every marriage will achieve optimum success, that no one will ever experience feelings of being lonely, that a rosy glow of happiness will prevail at all times. This just isn't the way life is. The important point to understand and to put into application is that life can be much less lonely and that marriage can be much more successful, if we rigorously convert all of our negativism to positivism, if we look into every situation, every phrase, every happening in life and extract from that the good intent that was probably behind it in spite of the way it sounds. When we recognize that the querulous or shrill voice that has irritated us sounds this way *not because of the person but in spite of the person,* when we recognize the fundamental goodness of everyone, when we recognize the constant demand placed upon us for a disciplined reaction to the other members of our family, when we see that our role is distinctly not one of taking from the family but one of giving, then that which will accrue to us can become abundant indeed.

Perhaps in summarizing this brief treatment of a unified, dynamic family life it is important to bring out that the total mission of the family must be defined. Decide that the mission of your family is going to be one of living gracefully, not graciously, in the stereotyped urban sense of the word, but to live gracefully, to exemplify the practice, to radiate the true meaning of grace. *And*—have some laughs! Humor is healthy, wholesome and can make of life a good thing! And perhaps in an even truer, more pervasive and meaningful way the meaning of grace as taught by the Bible.

Whether you subscribe to the Koran, the Torah, or the Bible, the meaning of God's grace is essentially the same and it all boils down essentially to one word and that is "applied *love*."

Freedom from fear is, of course, a vital requirement in carrying out the mission of graceful living. The fulfillment of the basic needs for recognition, security, opportunity and belonging are also requirements. But these can best be done within a framework of total family planning which calls for the definition of the mission of the family, the clarification of the coordination required (which means *talk it out*), the refinement and clarification of values which places primary emphasis on working together, discussing together, the process of changing your whole life from what you are *against* to what you are *for,* the necessity of rising above petty irritations and self-preoccupation, to being able to provide forgiveness even when it's rough and grudging and hard to do, the ability to graciously and warmly accept forgiveness so that the forgiver does not feel awkward, to be able to warmly and graciously accept an apology so that the person apologizing feels better, not worse, because of the apology, the determination to saturate this total plan, this set up of practices, principles and attitudes with the total process of faith and love here are the secrets. They are with you at all times. We are providing here no magic panacea, no pat formula. We are simply reviewing, helping to organize, helping to knit together into a total fabric called the unified, dynamic family life, a pattern of philosophy, principles, attitudes and values which can be a strong and tough sort of assurance as you proceed steadily to clear the rocky road and convert it into a smooth highway of family harmony.

While on a recent plane trip from New York to Chicago, I began chatting with an attractive, superbly dressed woman in her late 'forties. She told me her husband was a highly successful physician and she had just been visiting with their only daughter who had just started her third year in an exclusive women's college.

"You'd think I would be the happiest woman in the world, wouldn't you?" She said, "I've got more of everything luxurious than I ever yearned for as a child, my husband is a hard working, decent and respectable man and is looked up to by many people. I'm sure everybody in our community thinks we are happy indeed. Happy? I'm wretched! I feel empty and unnecessary. Who needs me? My husband is apparently in love with his work and that's all he wants. He has the silly notion that romantic words and physical love-making is not for 'middle-aged' people. Good heavens, I'd quickly give up everything we own if I could get back the vital feeling we used to have when we were together. Yes! I wish he was ardent and responsive again. We're not a family now—we're two expensively maintained individuals who are going to become two old relics."

It was obvious that a loving and tender partner was far more important to her than any amount of money. They needed unity —they needed oneness—they needed totality and integration. They needed, as the wedding service itself so often puts it, to *cleave* to each other. But the ceremony isn't enough. Tenderness, thoughtfulness, restraint, empathy, compassion, these are all the stuff of enduring love and unity—*but*—this fiber in the carpet will *never become knitted and unified until each partner* literally loves his or her spouse more than himself—and shows it! The act of love must be the sacrament of the total marriage.

While browsing in the paperback section at an airport, I recently read an article urging men to "take" their wives assertively and authoritatively. It was suggested that this was the sure way to bolster one's feelings of masculinity and to heighten the wife's feelings of helplessness and femininity. I put the article down wondering how many of its readers, uncertain of their manhood, might consider this a mandate for sheer exploitation of their biological urges and result in further blotting out a true exchange of *giving*—of reciprocal tenderness, of shared emotions, of true oneness. The further diminishing or elimination of this vital exchange between two souls who needed to become blended could easily increase the feelings of inadequacy of both the "taker" and the "taken." There is no substitute for total giving. Only by *losing* yourself (in total attention to the other) do you *find* yourself. (Here, incidentally, is the complete prescription for the fragmented existentialist who scurries desperately through life seeking to discover himself.)

Steps for Accomplishment

1. Do not refer to *my* house, *my* car, *my* son, etc. Realize and reflect that these things are *ours*—not *mine*. This helps you—requires you—to think and operate as a team rather than on a superior-subordinate basis.

2. When a wife has a tendency to feel menial in picking up after her husband—in endeavoring to please his unpredictable taste at mealtime, etc., she should recognize instead that these are symptoms of his *need* for her. Certainly, none of us is perfect—and he will certainly become progressively less perfect if you see all of his weaknesses as deliberate. Recognize that a weakness exists because of an unfilled need. It is equally vital for the husband, when he comes home in the evening, to find something to praise, or at least to comment on, which helps his wife over the awareness, she so often has anyway, of a day of imperfect achievement. Look for the strengths and dwell on them—the weaknesses will then begin to diminish.

3. Some women create an imbalance in the use of their time and may seem to spend too much time in activities outside the home. Let's put the big lens here on the husband and the children—we challenge you to show her in innumerable ways how *important* she is to you *at home*. Often, she has gotten over-involved outside the home simply because she doesn't feel sufficiently *needed*. Let her know!

4. Tragically often the "middle-aged" couple have lost the vital spark. Physical contact becomes increasingly rare. They provide only for

each other's material needs—food, home, paycheck, etc. Thus they may figuratively, or literally, begin to dry up and withdraw from the pulsating game called life. What to do?

a. Sit down and *talk it out*. Recognize bluntly that one—or maybe both—no longer seems to thrill to the other's touch as much as formerly.
b. Determine *why* & *when*.
c. Get a thorough physical—insure that glands and other vital organs are healthy.
d. Thoroughly recall and discuss the kinds of situations and circumstances that have been most joyous and fulfilling in past years.
e. Discuss very specifically the things that originally attracted you to each other. Things like appearance, touch, sound, smell, place, etc.
f. Your biggest obstacles will be prudishness, stereotypes, inhibition, ill-grounded puritanism, lack of sound basic information, old wives tales, and failure to recognize that well-directed and sanctified passion has much more virtue in the eyes of God than passiveness. The Bible itself states: "Wives, submit yourselves unto your own husbands, as unto the Lord."
g. By this time the situation should begin to resolve itself. If not—consult professional counsel.
h. Temptations to lapse into semi-comfortable and lazy passivity will continue to exist.

Dare to live passionately! ! ! !

11

THE "TOUGH-MINDED" SQUARE

Return of the Square

"Square," another of the good old words, has gone the way of "love" and "modesty" and "patriotism."

Something to be snickered over or outright laughed at.

Why, it used to be that there was no higher compliment you could pay a man than to call him "a square-shooter."

The adman's promise of a "square deal" once was as binding as an oath on the Bible.

But, today a "square" is a guy who volunteers when he doesn't have to.

He's a guy who gets his kicks from trying to do a job better than anyone else.

He's a boob who gets so lost in his work he has to be reminded to go home.

A square is a guy who doesn't want to stop at the bar and get all juiced up because he prefers to go to his own home, his own dinner table, his own bed.

He hasn't learned to cut corners or goof off.

This creep we call a "square" gets all choked up when he hears children singing "My Country 'tis of thee . . ."

He even believes in God—and says so—in public!

Some of the old squares were Nathan Hale, Patrick Henry, George Washington, Ben Franklin.

Some of the new squares are Glenn, Grissom, Shepard, Carpenter, Cooper, Schirra.

John Glenn says he gets a funny feeling down inside when he sees the flag go by. Says he's proud that he belonged to the Boy Scouts and the YMCA.

How square can you get?

A square is a guy who lives within his means whether the Joneses do or not, and thinks his Uncle Sam should, too.

He doesn't want to fly now and pay later.

A square is likely to save some of his own money for a rainy day, rather than count on using yours.

A square gets his books out of the library instead of the drugstore.

He tells his son it's more important to play fair than to win. Imagine!

A square is a guy who reads scripture when nobody's watching, and prays when nobody's listening.

A guy who thinks Christmas trees should be green and Christmas gifts should be hand-picked.

He wants to see America first—in everything.

He believes in honoring father and mother and "do unto others" and that kind of stuff.

He thinks he knows more than his teen-ager knows about car freedom and curfew.

Will all gooney birds answering this description please stand up.

> *You Misfits in this brave new age, you dismally disorganized, improperly apologetic ghosts of the past, stand up!*
> *Stand up and be counted!*
> *You squares . . . who turn the wheels and dig the fields and move mountains and put rivets in our dreams.*
> *You squares . . . who dignify the human race.*
> *You squares who hold the thankless world in place.*
>
> (From a broadcast by Paul Harvey—based on the address by Charles H. Brower, President of Batten, Barton, Durstine and Osborn, Inc.)

The "Tough-Minded" Square

By now it must have become obvious that the tough-minded individual has very little time and very little patience with those who simply focus upon their own selfish desires. Very little patience with those who hide behind the excuse of avant-garde intellectualism as a crutch to avoid the sometimes brain-wrenching, soul-twisting process of continuous study, continuous learning about the very practical business of living a totally successful existence. Very little patience with those who propound the "cult of imperfection" as a tranquil refuge. Fancy sounding phrases those? Well, they simply mean that the person who has decided that his mind will stay flexible, must stay young and ever-changing, that he may well be learning more rapidly at the age of 65 than he was at the age of 50, or that he will be learning more rapidly and achieving more at the age of 40 than he presently is at the age of 30.

This is the person whose mind continues to strengthen, to expand, to develop tough and sinewy dimensions. This is a person who does *not* feel it is *square* (in the most offensive modern use of the term) to want to make this life one of *total achievement*.

He has the basic wish and purpose, the goal, of leaving the earth a better place than he found it. The tough-minded square becomes a student of our free enterprise system and all that it denotes. He becomes an expert on our Constitution. He knows the Declaration of Independence applies to all people everywhere. (Did you know this? Re-read it. You may be surprised.) He masters thoroughly all of the basic and incomparable laws spelled out crisply and clearly in the New Testament. He has the capacity, the resilience and the ability to bounce back from defeat. He believes that it is easy to sound "tough-minded" when everything is going for you. He knows that it is easy to espouse integrity when there are no temptations in your way. But this tough-minded square, this guy who insists in leading an unusual life, an uncommon life of achievement and success, is the man who experiences some of his finest moments when the temptation to deviate from integrity is great and the adversities in terms of financial reverses, illness, death and other of life's major pitfalls occur. He knows that every problem can become a challenge. He focuses not on the weaknesses of people, but on their budding and potential strengths.

A tough-minded square is the man or woman who reflects all the habits, attitudes, values and beliefs stressed throughout this entire book. He insists upon learning more about them. He charges ahead with a smile, with a zest and a passion for life with all pores open to assimilate knowledge and insists, furthermore, upon the pragmatic application of this knowledge.

People used to point with some pride and pleasure to another individual and say: "He's a square-shooter. He earns three square meals a day. He stands four-square. He's a square guy." You know what kind of a guy this fellow was? He was corny and square enough to believe that there was something honorable and fine about hard work. If he was on the farm, he thought there was something to feel proud of if he could throw more bundles and scoop more grain. If he worked in a clothing store he thought it was great to be able to sell more clothes than somebody else. If he was a bank teller, he thought it was more important to get there early and leave late and build a reputation at the bank through sound service and he thought there was nothing to apologize about in this. In short, he felt that work was fine and good. This man was corny and square enough that he put the flag out on the 4th of July. This kind of a man used to get a lump in his throat when he saw a parade going by and he saw the flag. You see, he was really a square; he was really corny.

He believed his children should be equipped with deep, practicing religious faith. If he was a Christian, he believed that his children should understand and attempt very hard to emulate the teachings of Christ. If he was a Confucionist, he felt that a thorough understanding of Confucionism and its application to modern problems of living were understood and practiced.

You see, this guy was really square and he was really corny, but he was a pretty wonderful guy to be with and he was a successful man. He was a positive and tough-minded man.

A square is the man who is fit, wants to work hard, wants to walk tall with integrity and wants to reach out and build and give —who's got guts, who wants to move, who knows where he's going to go and the hipsters had better stay out of his way. The hipster, on the other hand, is the guy who thinks you can get something for nothing, who knows what he's against instead of what he's for.

I asked Beth Windsor, "The Girl Next Door," to express her views on the much discussed younger generation of budding adults. Beth is a 20 year old honor student at the State University of Iowa. She writes:

> Attending a huge university in this day can be a rather upsetting experience. As soon as the lost-feeling little freshman first steps out into the "campus atmosphere," he is bombarded by a number of phenomena which are a good deal more frightening than the traditional homesickness and "social insecurity" which have always faced the new student in his first weeks away from home. Now there are iconoclastic professors ready to topple childlike beliefs and values. There are large classes full of unknown faces and the newcomer feels more completely alone than he has ever felt before. But most appalling of all, there are strange atti-

tudes and ideas which must be confronted for the first time and somehow conquered. The most dangerous of these dark and formless threats are embodied in the "beat" or so-called "intellectual set" which haunts virtually every U.S. campus today.

Garbed in 20th century "sackcloth and ashes," these desolate looking figures mourn the death of positive hope, both intellectual and spiritual. With their dirty bodies, unorthodox dress, and vacant eyes, they impress the newcomer to the campus as having some nebulous, intellectual "answer" to all the world's problems. As he fits himself into the university community, the new student may ridicule these "beats," or, far more tragically, he may join them. Whatever his reaction, he is affected by their presence.

And what of the "answer" to virtually every problem that these "protesters" have found? In most cases, it is very simple and easy to put into practice. It is a sort of immobile retreatism which says: "The world can never be as we think it should be, so we choose to withdraw from its turbulence." Many truly intelligent "beats" have given their world a tremendous amount of thought. But in so doing, they have thought themselves into a state of stagnation. They have become incapable of positive action. Contemplating the "inevitable" is far easier than daring to try to change it.

When these "hollow men" do speak out, it is with a negative, hopeless voice. "All human movement is futile," they contend, "so let's not move." Even when these people do move, it is rarely on their own initiative. Usually, at the front of every bearded, stringy-haired "protest" group, there is a truly brilliant mind who has managed to stir up response to his cause. However, the positive aspect of the movement is still his. It is hardly ever original with the mutely hopeless protesters who carry his placards. The sad reality is that these "children" of the Atomic Era actually have no answer and no purpose. What they are really protesting is their own failure to find a way to live in the sometimes terrifying real world.

Many of these sensitive and intelligent people think they have found an escape from the difficulties of that world in what they like to call "non-conformity." The shaky theory behind this escape measure is that if one dresses, behaves, speaks, and thinks in ways which are not common within the society, then he is not a part of that society, and does not have to share the blame for the direction in which that society is moving. Given the behavior of most of the "beats," there are at least two fallacies in this theory. First, the external "non-conformity" in which they indulge is actually very rigid conformity. Who among the "initiated" would dare take a bath, shave, or comb his hair, or depart from the "beat" type of dress. The second flaw in this outlook is far more serious. It involves the sadly mistaken idea that one can completely separate himself from the society of which he is a product. The bearded ones haven't broken with our society, but rather, they are a frightened symptom of an ill which may be at work deep within its very heart. Their emptiness is a reflection of the emptiness—the lack of an inner strength—which threatens us all. It makes one shudder to think of the consequences if their hopeless negativism should spread.

What then, ultimately, is the solution for the student who is thoughtful and sensitive about the world around him, but who chooses *not* to follow the barren road of the "beat generation?" From the observations of one university student at least, it seems that the answer is to find, somewhere, the inner stamina to take the tremendous dare that the Atomic Age holds out.

The first place to seek this necessary stamina is within one's self. A positive self-evaluation in which the individual emphasizes his strong characteristics, and recognizes (but does not dwell upon his weak points) is the initial step to finding inner strength. Another source of such fortitude is a firm belief in a supreme power much larger than self. This "hooking up" to a wellspring of strength provides the basis for the final "action" phase of the search for the personal courage that our age demands. This is a projection of the individual's new-found stamina, outward, so that it reaches other human beings. It is a sharing or giving of one's own self which is beneficial for both the giver and the receiver. Going through this vital process is more important to the newcomer to the campus than any part of his university orientation. For, as the new student faces a large university, and later the world itself, he must develop the courage and the will to think and to act with a positive hope for tomorrow.

Beth, a vital, sparkling girl, *lives* the principle of passionate commitment.

I have blasted the currently prevalent concept of intellectualism which seems to say,

"We are the generation of the unwashed—the Nihilists, the Existentialists.

"Our creed is negativism: we are frightened, we are seeking identity, we are avant-garde claspers of Zen Buddhism, we hide our compulsive self-preoccupied fears behind a facade of 'intellectualism' and esoteric terminology. Basically, we are lazy and gutless."

Who needs these people? We do, our country does—because, while we have many emotional and intellectual pygmies—throughout the nation and the world—we can most certainly help them to change significantly and make a much greater contribution to mankind through the application of the techniques of tough-minded, successful living. Do *you* have the courage to do a bit of crusading the rest of your life and help to illuminate and/or enlighten some of these befuddled people who seem dedicated to imperfection and degeneracy. They are this way *in spite* of themselves—not *because* of themselves.

Is Graciousness Tough? The tough-minded square defines grace in the following way: "a special warmth felt and expressed toward all other human beings; an absence of pettiness and concern, a living manifestation of the belief that man should devote his major energies to doing something *for* others and not *to* others." Get rid of any possible confusion about the words "graciousness" and "tough." They are virtually synonymous for this reason: The great theologian and writer, Dr. Elton Trueblood, describes Christ Himself—who is considered to be the epitome of grace, of graciousness among mortals, as first of all "tough."

He said in a recent address that Christ was probably the toughest man who ever lived, that the concept of "Sweet Jesus, meek and mild" is as ungrounded in fact as any popular fallacy has ever been. Here was a man who radiated, taught and exemplified an inner grace through an all-out, unimpeded mission to give and build to provide warmth and direction, inspiration and "the way and the light." This was grace at its highest and best. Such grace would have been absolutely impossible without a tough mind and spirit which enabled Him to stand up fearlessly to a pattern of abuse and assault, innuendo, gossip, verbal vilification and physical abuse such as no man has ever been asked to submit to since that time.

The only way to move through life is in a gracious way, stimulating the hearts and minds of those who come in contact with us, giving them a lift of spirit, a tendency to view us as leaders rather than pushers, as inspirers rather than simply as hard bosses, or as wonderful spouses and mates rather than simply cold, hard, self-centered individuals. This type of graciousness we see as possible only—through a *spirit* that can weather—through a state of mind—that can weather the buffeting, the blows, the challenges, the reverses of modern living. There is probably no difference in the truly tough-minded person and the truly gracious person and I urge you to square away and to resist the fallacy of thinking of graciousness as simply "sweetness and light" which seemingly defers to the dignity of others, but which in reality ignores it.

The only way in which we give other individuals with whom we associate a full credit for complete, individual dignity is to interact with them in an atmosphere of complete truth. While there is never any excuse to deviate from truth, there is a tremendous and constant need for increased skill in how to use the truth. Many people, perhaps the majority of us, look for a crutch, for an excuse to keep from living with a total pattern of truth by using the excuse: "Oh, I've just got to tell a little white lie in this particular connection." What we are saying when we do this is simply this —that we have not taken the time and trouble to discipline our minds and develop sufficient skill in presenting the truth so that its impact will be thoroughly positive and helpful. In short, to live this way do you have the *self-discipline?* Do you have the *guts?* **Only *you* can answer.**

Steps for Accomplishment

1. *Live* integrity, rather than relying on preachments. Integrity is what you are, not what you say. Do you recall the old saying "What you *are* speaks so loudly, I can't hear what you are saying?" A prime example of this, of course, is the parent who preaches integrity, who requires integrity from his child but who practices something that could be labeled dubiously and at best as "adequate integrity." Every member of society with whom you come in contact must be able to fairly quickly recognize, sense and *know* that you are a person who insists on—and settles for nothing less— than the application of truth in all things.
2. In all community activities insist upon focusing not simply upon the activity with which you are engaged or the activity with which other people attempt to impress their neighbors and community associates, but rigorously reach for and insist upon clarifying and outlining the end results which you hope to achieve by this community action. Then, relate all organization, all action and all activity to these results and pay no attention and waste no energy upon diffused and aimless activity.
3. Practice candor and warmth widely, deeply and continuously.
4. Have the guts to say what ought to be said. Realize that the time for permissiveness, pussyfooting and obsequious cringing, crawling behavior is a thing of the past. The person who is going to achieve true success, truly big things in life *has got to hold such a sound and worthwhile opinion of himself that he can reach out to others* confidently with a complete lack of permissiveness and communicate to them crisply, precisely, and passionately what he can *give* them and what he expects from them in order to achieve sizeable and significant achievements.
5. Have as one of your principal objectives as a member of society the thorough absorption, understanding and simplification of all of the principles of tough-minded living. There is no better way to help others than to first of all exemplify the precepts of tough-mindedness and to require from others, then, the type of behavior which lives up to these standards.
6. Be a humanitarian, but do not waste needless time on carrying out

stereotyped "do gooder" activities. Make sure you are not attempting simply to kid yourself as an excuse to read your name in the paper.
7. Recognize that "business by integrity" can be a rallying point for true social, political and economic progress.
8. Focus upon the strengths of political and municipal officials, rather than simply commenting caustically on their weaknesses. The latter course will achieve you nothing but a dull, gray feeling, frustration and stomach ulcers. Whereas, a focus upon the strengths of these people holds the one real possibility of improving the situation in a realistic and lasting manner.
9. Recognize that it takes more courage and ability to strengthen our society than it takes to highlight its weaknesses.
10. When broad problems are presented, do not be content to simply talk within an appointed committee. Request target dates, set them, define objectives and, then, carry out *action*.

What we do upon some great occasion will probably depend on what we are; and what we are will be the results of previous years of self-discipline.

H. P. LIDDON

12

THE WINNING EDGE— DISCIPLINE OF SELF

Be a Giant, Not a Pygmy

The need for giants rather than mental and spiritual pygmies in our country today is certainly obvious and manifest when you examine just a few of our major newspapers and magazines. A number of people who seem to be fleeing from life, who fear to take a stand, who fear to use discipline, who simply look for refuge from their fears and from the complexities and anxieties of modern living, through drunkenness, through extra-marital affairs, through crime and delinquency, appears to be on a steady and rapid increase. (*Note:* Don't lose sight of the many fine young people coming along. They are there—just *look!*)

It is well established by now that the weak personality—hard, unchanging, and rigid—is the person who indulges himself in excessive drinking, compulsive eating, and other anxiety-driven manifestations. He is the person to feel sorry for, to feel compassion for, and to try and convert from small, scurrying, hurrying, pygmy-like activities to a tall, mental and spiritual giant who walks with easy strides through life and who is able to transcend the petty fears and anxieties of day-to-day living and convert this to positive, unhurried serenity and accomplishment.

Develop a list which represents all of the solid and positive things you want to accomplish in life and look at this two or three times a week. Check off each day those things which you are moving solidly toward, and look hard at those which you are failing to make measurable progress toward. For example, such objectives are: You resolve to attempt to understand your boss if he tends to reprimand you excessively or you feel he "has it in for you." First of all, recognize very clearly and simply and practically that, as a rule, no normal boss is trying to criticize or seek to get rid of any employee who is making him more successful. Thus, you need to first search yourself and make sure that your activities day after day are designed to make him more successful and are designed to help him receive the results of his job, are designed to provide him with reassurance concerning his basic ability, his worth and, perhaps most importantly of all, your loyalty to him.

If you work hard and diligently at demonstrating these particular things, you will seldom ever find cause to feel that you are being "picked on." If, in spite of such diligent efforts at contributing to his success you still tend to find that you suffer from a feeling of persecution, you may be working for an individual who has deep-seated problems which do not meet the eye. Attempt then to rise above the petty considerations, the fears, irritations and frustrations which you have been experiencing, and try desperately to understand him better and to allow for this behavior. Many times in this way your own example will tend to help eradicate the troublesome situation. If, in spite of carrying out these two disciplined patterns of action, you find no real improvement, then it is perhaps best for you to change positions. In certain instances the man and his job are simply mismated no matter what you may attempt to do. This can well be called a planned and positive change for the better.

Take a Deep Breath

If we do not basically feel well, we will not work well, think well, or look well. Thus our entire life becomes colored. Wherever we go, we begin to build around us a climate of negativism, cynicism, and sometimes, accompanying neurosis and weakness. The tough-minded person who will settle for nothing less than full success as a full man or woman, develops a thorough check list concerning his health habits. Here are some sample questions to ask:

1. Are you getting adequate exercise? Is it the kind of exercise that makes your blood race through your veins? It makes you breathe hard, it makes you pump oxygen out to your fingertips, it puts new color in your cheeks. Are you doing this every day, systematically and well? If you're under 50, ask your physician for clearance and guidance to exercise the equivalent of running two miles each day.
2. Are you avoiding excessive carbohydrates and saturated fats? Are you trying to eat a balanced diet high in protein, minerals and the essential vitamins? Read the books of Ancel Keys, Lelord Kordel and Gayelord Hauser.
3. Do you insist upon getting the necessary sleep? Many people require from 8 to 10 hours. For others 6 hours is sufficient. Be sure and find your particular requirement and then make every effort to get a complete night's sleep each night of the week.
4. Make sure that you have the discipline over your drives and hungers so that you do not drink to excess. Anything in excess of one or two cocktails or one or two beers per day must be considered excess for the clear-eyed, clear-minded, success-oriented individual.
5. Smoking, of course, is completely out the window. Any person who stops and reads just a bit of the objective, carefully compiled literature prepared by both our government and research organizations, cannot possibly continue to smoke and main-

tain a serene conscience that acts positively to preserve and build a fit body which is a suitable temple for a clear and tough mind. *You decide!*

The Trim Silhouette

Take a look in the mirror. If you can get hold of any surplus flesh around your middle so that there is over a half inch between your thumb and forefinger, you've got a problem and a challenge. Many have found the exercise routine prescribed by the Royal Canadian Air Force as being quite suitable for all ages, since this is a carefully worked out formula that provides for a gradual increase which is related closely to the individual's age, starting condition and capacity for steady improvement. I have found it significant to notice in discussing and working with top executives and top professional people throughout our country that very few truly successful people appear to be anything but trim, fit, and squared away for action. Such people have usually discovered the legacy of ill health, hangovers and half-baked accomplishment which follows over-indulgence in eating, drinking and the lack of a clearly worked out and stretching and pulse-pounding program of physical exercise. Remember, you are only competing with yourself. Don't fret over comparing yourself with others.

Optimum mental alertness is simply not possible without a lean and fit body.

A Profile of Self—Believe In Yourself! ! ! !

Do you have the courage to sit down in front of a full length mirror and take in a long unblinking appraisal of yourself? Many of us shy away from this particular kind of candid, all revealing look because our face does not resemble that of Rock Hudson or Gina Lollobrigida; or the ladies discover that they do not have the lovely shoulders and swan-like neck that they would like to believe they have. The men discover that they do not have the physique, the chiseled-profile, etc. of some of the better known, handsome, leading men. There is no real merit, as we have brought out time and again, in dwelling on your weaknesses. We're all pretty much aware of these. But in terms of recognizing how we can make our appearance an asset, rather than a liability, we first need to take a long look at just where we are in this particular point in time. If we need to trim down, if we need to straighten up, if we need to lift our chin, lift our head, stick out chest, pull in our abdomen, and walk tall— then we had better be aware of this so we can rigorously set out to do so. If we have a habit of rolling our eyes or twitching our lips or any of these particular habits, again it behooves us to know what we are doing so that we can change for positive improvement immediately. Thus, the importance of taking a periodic audit of our own self profile is obvious and manifest if we are to continue to progress step-by-step toward total fitness of mind, body, spirit and develop a unity and oneness of personality that enables us to propel ourselves onward and upward toward the kind of success that gives us real dignity and a real feeling of accomplishment as total individuals.

Do you want to become flabby, soft, red-eyed and blubbery? Want your chest to fall? Want to lose your sexual vigor and attractiveness? Here are some proven ways:

1. Stoke up on pies, cakes, doughnuts, potatoes, bread and malted milks whenever your energy is low. Scrupulously avoid lean meat, eggs, crisp green vegetables and buttermilk! In his great book *Eat Your Troubles Away* (World Publishing Co., 1955), Leland Kordel writes: "Recently a group of sexually normal men participated in an experiment in which they were fed extremely low amounts of proteins. They satisfied their appetites with high-starch meals. They were surprised to find they had lost all interest in women—even when the opposite sex paraded past them on the bathing beaches or allowed their dresses to fly up at windy corners. Female curves did not appeal to these normal males who had been protein-starved."
2. When you feel like exercising, lie down until the notion passes away.

3. Assume that only a sissy insists on a full night's sleep.
4. Find your "kicks" in soft drinks, beer, and liquor.
5. Become sensitive, resentful and conforming if your pot-bellied friends criticize you for any occasional symptoms of dynamism or health-consciousness. Follow—don't lead.
6. Consider boredom and tranquility to be synonymous. Boredom is truly deadly and can push you toward your debility goals in a hurry.
7. Shun your annual physical and label it as "sissy stuff." Assume doctors are jerks.
8. Assume that a "real" man gives vent to many displays of temper and incentive.
9. Kid yourself that the world loves a fat man. Women don't. The foregoing nine statements are not complete, but if you follow them faithfully we can pretty much guarantee you a substantial and continuing amount of misery.

Attitudes Are the Key

We are in a very real sense a product of our attitudes. If we *think* we are little people, we are going to *be* little people. If we *think* we are losers, we are going to *be* losers. If we think we are average, status quo individuals, this is precisely what we are going to *be*. If, on the other hand, we determine that we are going to *achieve* abundance and we're going to cram every hour of wakeful living in our years on this planet with *achievement, giving, building,* and *savoring* of all that life provides, we can certainly do this. There is absolutely no doubt that, *if we decide we are going to condition our attitudes totally toward success, we can do it!* Recognizing that even though we will experience periodic failures and periodic setbacks until the day we die, the whole point is that we pay little attention to these when they happen, because we have so completely focused upon what *can* be done, what is *going* to be done, what *will* be done, what *must* be done, that we have no time and patience for our own occasional doubts, our own occasional setbacks. These we relegate into the limbo of insignificant, inconsequential nothings.

The Practical Man

I have been particularly unimpressed with a number of legislators in our nation's capital who look blurry-eyed and paunchy and might consider it an impractical waste of time to concentrate on anything other than (and this is often their excuse) "legislation." This is typical, also, of a number of leaders in business.

Admittedly they are a distinct minority, those who are many times only hovering on the periphery of real success. But so often we hear from some of these pseudo-successful people that "I'm too busy getting the important things done, I'm a practical man, I don't have time to concentrate upon my own personal health." They are saying, in effect, that they are noble martyrs to the cause of practical achievement. This is usually rank nonsense. The bald fact is that in most of these cases the individual simply lacks the discipline, the dedication, or concern for others which is required in whipping himself into a top-notch level of mental preparation, a level of emotional harmony which helps him provide to his associates, to his subordinates, to his superiors, to his family members, a healthy mind which is reaching out and providing others with warmth, reassurance and aid in their own particular programs of success. This is the man who not only uses self-discipline, but has the wisdom to continue to use it and continue to cultivate a greater measure of this discipline because he knows that true happiness, true success, vibrant, clear-eyed healthy, a full-packed, inquisitive and ever-growing mind is about as "practical as one can ever get." *He does not flee from success!* (Read "The Hound of Heaven" by Francis Thompson.)

You Are No More Alive Than You Look

Stand on a busy street corner downtown some day and start looking closely at the people who walk by. How many of them are well groomed? How many of them have their chests out? How many of them look as though life were a great adventure? How many of them look as though real pleasure, real challenge, real achievement is just around the corner. You'll find that one in every one hundred at best gives this appearance. Or, it would be probably more realistic in the average metropolitan center to say that one in every thousand. But, when you see this kind of person, notice that you feel a little bit better yourself. You feel a little bit more stimulated by the challenges of your own day. Imagine then what kind of environment this particular person builds around him. He is stacking the cards one hundred per cent in his favor because when he looks at his business or professional associates with a ready smile, with a quick handshake, with a constant radiation of warmth, with a clear-eyed inquiry into the interests, desires and goals of others and a ready desire to help them achieve them, you can count in a very realistic and practical sense on the fact that this man cannot be thwarted in his drive for success. He cannot be thwarted because he knows what he's *for* and all the people with whom he associates, with just a few exceptions, are going to help in subtle ways, many times unconsciously, to push him right up into the major role in life that he is building for himself.

Spiritual Power

In *Romans 8:31* we find the phrase, "If God be for us, who can be against us." Here we see one of the key sources for spiritual power. I challenge you to imagine that you are filled, pulsating and radiating with this invisible but very definite power. Go through the following three steps: *visualize, synthesize, energize.* What is that elusive something that we call the spirit? We know that it possesses the power to turn common people into uncommon people. To transform mundane, meaningless lives into lives of searching power, purity and purpose. We know that it is perhaps the most essential ingredient in the person who experiences total success but it is very difficult to isolate. This is because it is all pervasive, it reaches out and saturates everything and everybody with whom we come in contact. Here is a little exercise to give you some actual, practical insight into the surging potential power lying dormant within you at the moment.

Go through the New Testament and make a list of every sentence which contains the word "faith," and then underline each of these sentences and have each of them typed up separately. Then, sit down and read this list once a day, every day, for three weeks. See what happens. Your own testimony at the end of a year of this is going to amaze you and all of your friends around you. You will discover as you continue to pore over these great, powerful and positive truths that the universe, the world, the entire living environment created by God were all conceived in perfect order and perfect harmony. You will find in studying the animals that roamed the woods in a nondomesticated state an essential harmony with nature, a total blending in with the total sweep and swirl and flawless hurrying along of nature. You will perceive, in short, that the only thing which seems to fly in the face of nature, which seems to charge about in meaningless frenetic activity, is the human race.

The vast majority of us seek to find, simply within our own minds, environments, and society, the entire answer to the challenge of living a full and successful life in our contemporary world. *The time for this is long since past.* It behooves each of us to make a study of the essential unity and harmony of all of the laws and principles which surround us. These can be found through a thorough study of all of the articles dealing with faith in the New Testament. Here are a set of principles which are in perfect harmony. No scholar since the beginning of civilized man has ever been able to find one inconsistency, one flaw, one inharmonious statement in the entire New Testament.

I challenge each of you as people poised at the beginning of a real adventure in stimulating, dynamic living to wade in to this New Testament with a very curious mind, with the feeling that you are going to experience the greatest story ever written, the greatest mental and emotional adventure you have ever undertaken, the greatest eye-opening, soul-awakening, pulse-quickening, series of findings that you have ever encountered. Give it a real go and see what happens.

It is popular to say, "The spirit is willing, but the flesh is weak." Baloney! The truth is in most cases that "the flesh is willing but the spirit is weak."

Build spiritual power and it's amazing how the body responds to almost superhuman requirements. Learn, through step-by-step discovery, to blend the laws of God and man and few obstacles can daunt you.

Don't Confuse Activity with Results

Throughout this nation we see a multitude of scurrying men and women who seem to be trying desperately to impress their bosses with how busy they are. Many times these people are quite apprehensive that they are not going to be fully compensated for this, that their salaries may not be what they think they should be—and they wonder why. Many times these people are also trying desperately to impress themselves with the feeling that they are doing something worthwhile, something that has basic dignity, something that has essential worth, by constantly being on the move. When they walk from one desk to another they move fast; when they walk down the hall they move fast. Sometimes you stop one of these persons and you say, "What are you getting done?" and they cannot tell you. What will *you* have achieved when you get down to the end of life's hall and transact your business? I can't tell you.

Sometimes we'll find the housewife, maybe with just one, two or three children, in the age of modern, mechanical gadgetry who seems to be constantly on a frenetic and frenzied merry-go-round and she says, "Oh, I'm so busy I don't have time to do this, I don't have time to do that." You say to her, "What are you getting *done?*" and she will often stop and say, "Well, I've just been telling you; I've been taking care of the kids. I've got to cook; I've got to take care of the house. I've got to participate in P.T.A. I've got to do this; I've got to do that." You again ask her, "What are you getting *done?*" I think you will find this little question to be very potent if you begin to ask yourself quite often, at least once a day, ideally about ten times a day, "I know what I'm *doing*, but the important thing is—what am I getting *done?*" We need, then, to make this life of ours meaningful, purposeful, successful and rich, to make sure that each of our days, each of our hours are filled with some kind of actual achievement instead of scurrying around and chasing our tails. We can and do wind up much more fatigued at the end of a day of frantic, purposeless activity than we do at the end of a day that has moved systematically from the half hour to the hour and hour by hour to a specifically planned-out set of *accomplishment* goals.

Promises for Untapped Power

A rich arsenal of untapped power exists in each of us. The average person is considered energetic and successful if he uses 20 per cent of his potential.

One of the most important missing ingredients is a crystal clear set of goals which give our lives meaning, sparkle, direction and fulfillment. And all this time a towering and bountiful set of goals exists for the taking. These are the 2,000 promises for us which are described beautifully and clearly in the New Testament. Think of that—*2000* promises for a life of almost unbelievable abundance, richness, power, beauty and excitement.

Make no mistake about it—our greatest arsenal for obliterating the fortress walls of self-preoccupation, mediocrity and misery, and helping all of those who seek a better life, is taken directly from the word of God—and from no other source.

The methods and techniques of teaching were developed and are being honed ever sharper, on the grindstone of experience—of vast contact with the futile efforts of thousands who have sought simply to buy or claw for real happiness. So, never forget— There are over *two thousand* promises waiting for you to claim! Do you have the discipline—do you have the *courage*—to unlock the door to your own vast spiritual reservoir and *really live?* Can you stand this pure and rarefied kind of success? Can you step up and over the threshold to your divine destiny?

The world desperately needs men and women who refuse to scurry through life half-alive, always fearful, usually futile. Every type of organized activity in the nation, indeed in the world, cries out for real leadership, real goals, real involvement, real commitment. All right! You can't lay this book down after a thoughtful reading without an awareness that you have been, and are, pointed toward the glistening heights of your potential. What are you going to *do* about it??

Happiness—A State of Mind

It is utterly nonsensical to tell you that you can create for yourself a condition of mind which will insure that all of your waking hours are one hundred per cent happy. This was purely and simply never a part of the total plan provided by the Creator. Unless we have downs, we cannot appreciate the ups. Unless we have a certain measure of tragedy, we cannot appreciate and savor the triumphs. We cannot learn from experience if we constantly experience nothing but success.

Life is a great equation; at the end of each life there are a number of negatives and a number of positives. The challenge before us, however, is not to accept this as something fatalistically that is going to happen, and therefore resign from the business of living and drift along without purpose. Let's make sure that when the final count adds up that the positives we have acquired are so large because we have faced up to and waded through some monumental negatives, that we have a strong and unshakeable testimony to having lived a life that is truly meaningful. *Never*, I repeat, *never*, hide behind the presence or lack of academic education as a crutch for failure to achieve a consistent pattern of happy, purposeful and abundant living. In the final analysis the real key is discipline of the self. Discipline comes from the word "disciples" and as anyone with elementary Sunday School information knows, the Disciples who followed Christ were people who believed in, followed, and sought to practice His teachings. Thus, if we provide our mind with all of the spiritual information with faith reinforcing power, this then gives us some very worthwhile goals with which to develop our daily emotions and purpose. In short, this requires of our mind a disciple-like approach to a set of goals which are bigger than we are. No matter how we grow, no matter how we progress, no matter how we change, we must always have goals just a little bit out of reach. This calls for discipleship, or discipline, of the most demanding but the most satisfying kind.

Recently the Sunday High School class at a Carlisle, Iowa Church, taught by Hal Batten, brother of one of the authors, was studying the Apostle Paul as one of the world's greatest writers. It was suggested that Craig Petre, President of the Youth Fellowship, write to Mr. D. H. Meenach of Dallas, Texas. Mr. Meenach is a wealthy businessman who began to practice his personal Christian faith while living in near poverty in Kentucky years ago. He was asked for any comments he cared to pass on to a class of High School students regarding a personal faith and personal success. The following letter was received in return:

Superior Foods, Inc.
Dallas, Texas

May 24, 1965

Dude H. Meenach,
President

Dear Craig:

How nice of you to write, and it was a very pleasant surprise for me to hear that Mr. Batten was so impressed by our one brief visit.

Yes, Craig, I do have a deep faith and belief in God. As I am dictating this letter, I am on my way from Dallas to Orlando, Florida, to speak on my favorite subject, "The Secret of Power." I am flying at 37,000 feet at a ground speed of nearly 600 miles per hour. Fifty years ago we would have called it a miracle to go from Dallas to Orlando in less than two hours, today, we call it jet plane travel. Without God, this could not be possible at all. We are using lots of God's unalterable laws to fly this plane. Gravity, motion, aerodynamics *and* above all faith. As I sit here enjoying this flight, I have complete faith in the pilot's ability and his God-given faith in himself that he can fly this plane.

You know the earth is just so far from the sun. If we were 1% closer, we would burn up, 1% farther away and we would freeze to death. The earth sets just right on its axis, and revolves at just the right speed. We orbit in a definite course. Is this by accident? I rather think not, God in his perfect way imagined this to be, just as he imagined you and I. We plant corn and up shoots a stalk, maybe mysterious to some, and it brings forth ears of corn and hundreds of tiny grains that can reproduce itself many, many times. I am positive there is a God, and the very best way to develop a real steadfast faith in Him is by daily using God's laws and principles in our daily life. Your life and the lives of those around you will be so good, healthful, prosperous and beautiful that your steadfast faith will just explode from you and others can't help but be affected by your faith.

You know Christ spoke the Aramaic language. I have a Bible that is translated from the Aramaic language. One of the verses in the New Testament says, "Get spiritual understanding and everything else will be added unto you." As a very young boy (12 years), I happened to read that and started immediately to search for spiritual understanding and knowledge. And, getting spiritual understanding was so simple to me, it is hard to believe. There are over 2,000 promises in the Bible, I believe every one of them, especially: "Ask, and it shall be given you; seek, and ye shall find, knock, and it shall be opened unto you. . . ."

We live under three sets of laws; they are all good and operate differently. Number one is "Man-made Laws." These are necessary for us in order for us to live together in society. Rarely a day goes by that nearly all of us violate some man-made law. I drove to my office this morning. The sign said 30 miles per hour, I just know I was driving 35, but I didn't get caught so nothing happened. We should always obey man-made laws, they too have their good purpose, but if we don't get caught nothing happens to us. Our second set of laws is "Physical Laws," or you could call them "Nature's Laws." We must obey them 100% all the time, or nothing happens. If we get in our cars and start the engine; and bear in mind, it has to have gas, the battery charged, all the wires connected, etc., or we could not even start it; anyway, start the engine but don't put it in gear and try to "pray" or "positive think" your way to town. You just won't get there, you are trying to violate a physical law and it won't work.

If we would get up on a high building and jump off and "pray" on our way down, we are going to be in trouble, because we would be asking God to revoke the immutable law of gravity and He won't and can't do it. Now, would it be smart to rationalize with ourselves half way down and say, "well, so far so good," we will hit the ground and be dead for certain. So, we all obey "Physical Laws," for the simple reason we are forced to do so.

Now, the third set of laws are "Spiritual Laws." Partially obeyed they give partial results. So, Craig, here you and I are, the sum total of our past obeyingness of "Spiritual Laws." If we want more good, health, wealth, happiness, then all we have to do is obey "Spiritual Laws" more. But, we have to know what these laws are before we can obey them, don't we? You know the old saying, "that things you don't know don't hurt you," is absolutely not true. Things we don't know do hurt us, because if we knew all the "Spiritual Laws" and obeyed them, then all the good we could possibly want would be ours now! Remember this, things we don't do hurt us more than the things we do.

By the very fact that you wrote, Craig, seeking advice, tells me that you are on your way. I'll certainly "bet" on Craig Petre, that he will accomplish *anything* he sets out to do. Get yourself a Bible translated from the Aramaic language and get into a *daily* habit of reading at least a chapter a day. Read mostly in the New Testament, you can read from random, no set order is necessary. I read my Bible early in the morning, when I first awake, while my mind is rested and clear and before the work day barges in, (I am in my 28th year of *daily* reading). After a while you will start understanding the Bible allegorically, getting meanings for you to apply in your daily life *now!* Don't ask me or anyone "why?" you don't need to know "why?" You and I don't know the "why?" of electricity but, we use it, don't we? (Not even the scientist understands electricity.) Don't worry about "why?" just start reading, and asking God for "Spiritual Understanding," you will get it and much sooner than you expect.

As you get more and more "Spiritual Understanding," and learning the "Spiritual Laws" and obeying them, then you will be a shining example and you by your way of life and the fact that you will really have *everything* you want, you will influence many, many people for good. You know we must all progress to really live. We must always go forward, more money, more good things in our life, yes, material things, more happiness. Never go backwards or stand still. To stand still is really living backwards. You know "LIVE" spelled backwards spells "EVIL"—it's a sin to be poor!

All your good has always been ready for you. You will receive it when you are mentally able to receive it. So, get the understanding, everything else will be added. I hear and read so much of you teenagers. Some nut is trying to convince me that you all are bad, I don't think so, and you have proven me to be right. As long as there is one Craig Petre left in this world then everything is going to be good, because it is teenagers like you that will accomplish so much good that thousands of others will follow your example.

Feel free to use my letter in any way you see fit—to accomplish your desire of wanting to know how teenagers can develop and use a steadfast faith in God.

I feel so good about meeting you via correspondence. Tell Mr. Batten a "hello" and "thank you" for me. Feel free to write me anytime. If in my travels I get near Carlisle, Iowa I will certainly look you up.

In His Name,
D. H. Meenach

To be a "tough-minded," disciplined person you should know that the disciplined mind is the happy mind. That planning is essential to happiness, but it takes courage and it takes personal discipline to make positive things happen and the disciplined way is the happy way. The undisciplined way is the confused way; the futile and meaningless way, the way of sorrows.

You should recognize that hardness is weak, because it is conditioned by hate. Recognize further that *love is the toughest and most powerful emotion in all the world!* This is an emotion when properly absorbed, when properly suffused throughout the body, mind and spirit—this is a source of power which very literally can move mountains. We current humans have only started to tap the potential and power of *love*—tough-minded *love!*

Resolve that you will never again think like a pygmy and whether your physical stature is four feet eleven, five feet six, or six feet five, that you will walk through life as a spiritual *giant.* Recognize that your total value as a person is nothing more nor less than the total values which you hold, believe and live. Say it with *passion* and with *power.* You should recognize that personal dignity is not what you say or how you look, but what you *are.* Recognize that the rebel knows what he's *against.* The individual knows what he is *for.* We all need a feeling of significance but the greatest way to obtain full significance is to recognize the significance of others and help build and expand this significance into a truly powerful spirit.

You need to recognize that the opportunities for growth and contribution in our country were never as great as now. They will continue to become greater unless we succumb to the bomb, through our failure as both a nation and as intellectual leaders of the world to *clarify our values.* If we continue to concentrate upon even more elaborate and sophisticated electronic mechanisms for destruction instead of the clarification and thorough communication and transmission of our values—the kind of values with which we have been highly concerned throughout this book—we may be sentencing ourself to our own crucifixion in the fiery hell of the nitrogen bomb. The tides of hate have built and washed about the world in recent years until they strongly threaten overcoming and suffusing all of mankind. This, we firmly believe, will never happen!!

The people of the United States as well as the other peoples of the world have an obligation to reach deep within their own spiritual, mental, and physical reservoirs and pull out the kind of resolve which will wrench this spinning world around away from an obsessive preoccupation with destruction and concentrate only upon building, creating, giving, expanding. So recognize that there are more big jobs than there are big men, but that you will become one of the big men or one of the big women to fill not only one of those big jobs, but to make it even bigger.

Feel and live your passion with sufficient depth to feel compassion for—not fear or contempt of—the new and not-so-new pallid people who forlornly cry "God is dead." There is no better medicine for lost and fragmented souls than love and truth piled in skillful and generous quantities.

Steps for Accomplishment

List under each category three ways to provide greater self discipline for yourself and then rate your progress for the next four weeks. A–Excellent, B–Good, C–Average, D–Fair, E–Poor. (See page 169.)

	1st week	2nd week	3rd week	4th week
Religion 1. 2. 3.				
Timeliness & Promptness 1. 2. 3.				
Health & Physical Appearance 1. 2. 3.				
Finances 1. 2. 3.				
Recreation 1. 2. 3.				
Personal Relationships 1. 2. 3.				
Service Organ- izations (Giving of Self) 1. 2. 3.				
Others that are appropriate for you.				

The great were once as you.
They whom men magnify today
Once groped and blundered on life's way
Were fearful of themselves and thought
By magic was men's greatness wrought.
They feared to try what they could do;
Yet fame hath crowned with her success
The selfsame gifts that you possess.

EDGAR A. GUEST

13 Know Thyself

BUILD ON YOUR STRENGTHS

"*Know thyself.*" It's an easy prescription, but one that is hard to carry out. Since it was first laid down by Socrates in ancient times, men have sought better ways of appraising themselves objectively. But there is no such thing as objective self-appraisal. The very concept of objectivity presupposes that a large enough number of people agree on a certain point. When appraising yourself, you can accept the opinions of others in terms of the impression you are making, but only you can determine whether or not you like what you see. Everyone reads you differently, sees a different facet of you. Therefore, you have to abandon the idea of going out and taking a vote.

There is a good chance that you know yourself better than you think you do. It's a matter of sitting down and listing your strengths and weaknesses. The main thing is to pull your thinking together and get it down in writing so that it doesn't keep sliding and slipping away from you. You begin defining yourself to yourself by taking a piece at a time.

First, you put down some of the more obvious things about yourself: for example, your age and other physical characteristics. Here you can throw in an evaluation of your total appearance and the impression you feel you make on people. Then you go on to describe your mental capacities, your ambitions, your energy level. You judge how persevering you are, how thoughtful and considerate. You state your physical stamina and well-being, the things you like and don't like, the times of the day you seem to work better than others, and why. It won't be long before you've developed a framework that will be a start at a self-description in terms of strengths, desires, and interests.

The second step is to develop an ability to observe yourself in the various dynamic processes of life—at work, in the home, with friends. A man is more what he does than what he thinks he is. And, however strange it may seem, he often becomes what he says and does even though it may be contrary to his basic desires. It is important to decide whether you are actually yourself or whether you are trying to be something that you are not. To observe yourself in action, so to speak, you develop what might be called a "calculated schizophrenia." This is not as difficult as it seems. You merely have to set aside a small part of your thinking apparatus and pretend you are looking over your own shoulder as you experience life. You will be able to do this quite easily if you will make it a habit to keep a day-to-day diary—not necessarily a lengthy or soul-searching document but just an accounting of what you observed yourself doing during the day, why you did it, how well it was done, and what kind of results you achieved.

What Others Think

The third important step in learning about yourself is to solicit the opinions of people with whom you are in contact in various situations. Find out what your wife thinks of you, what your business associates think of you, what your fellow church members think of you. Select a few men and women and ask them for an honest evaluation.

This may be a little embarrassing, but it should not be impossible if you make it quite clear what you are after. Take special care to choose people who have had the opportunity of observing and working with you in different ways and under different conditions. Keep a written record of their evaluations, jotting down a few notes the first chance you have.

It is only practical to recognize, however, that individuals see you through their eyes; they judge you against their standards. Therefore, don't be alarmed if you are never successful in portraying the same image to all the people you meet. It's only the basic things you stand for and believe in that you want them to recognize in you—integrity, candor, warmth, wisdom.

As you learn the knack of calculated schizophrenia, you will begin to develop greater empathy. This doesn't mean knowing how you would feel if you were in another man's shoes; it means knowing how you would feel if you were actually that other man with his knowledge, fears, biases, and desires. Empathy will grow rapidly if you strive hard to sense how people feel about a situation in which they are involved, how they react to you and how they react to other people. And with this greater empathy, with your new ability to read the impressions of your family, friends, and associates correctly, you will be better able to determine whether you are actually communicating what you want to communicate. You will truly begin to know yourself.

Accept Yourself

An even more important part of knowing yourself is the willingness to accept yourself. Sometimes this is far more difficult. All of us have a tendency not to be happy with what we are, to set standards for ourselves that are far greater than any we would set for others; as a result, we may be plagued constantly by feelings of guilt and frustration.

We must not only accept ourselves but also accept the basic fact that we will always be making mistakes. Unless we concede that we can fail and that failure does not mean total destruction of personality, we will never be able to achieve success and happiness. Nor will we ever be able to accept other people as they are and contribute to their success. Whenever we view ourselves as we are and then set out to define what we want to be, there will obviously be some gaps. The way to overcome these gaps is to select the one which we think is most important and to lay out a calculated plan for improving in this single area, recognizing that it may take time and that the important point is to make some progress each day.

Remember, we have to set our own standards. We have to arrive at our own conclusions and our own value system and then do our best to live accordingly. If the values and beliefs that we develop for ourselves do not fit in with our present environment —then we must go find the kind of environment in which we can act in accordance with those values and beliefs. It is only when we have achieved the spiritual independence which is bound to result that we can proceed to build on our strengths and the strengths of others.

**Focusing On Weaknesses
—The Road to Oblivion**

Are you pinched, pallid and putrid? You can reduce yourself to a timorous, quivering wreck of a person if you focus on what is wrong with you, what is wrong with members of your family and what is wrong with your school, your community, with your job, the people who work for you and for whom you work. This is the quick, guaranteed road to oblivion.

Did you ever notice that a champion livestock judge is noted primarily for his ability to sense perfect conformation or strong assets in a particular animal, rather than simply his ability to ferret out imperfections or poor conformation?

Have you ever noticed that the outstanding judge is not the person who has sent the most people to the electric chair, the hangman's noose or the prison, but the person who finds within the law of the land the obscure but positive interpretations which enable those who live within the law to live a more meaningful and challenging existence.

Time spent on analysis of what you can't do, of what you don't want to do, of what you are not qualified to do, in short, a complete focus upon negativism, is time completely and irretrievably lost. Decide that you are going to benefit from the experiences of thousands of others and vigorously and ruthlessly cast all negativism out of your life.

Focusing on weaknesses is the comfortable thing to do. There is no stretch—no challenge—only neuroticism and mediocrity. Most few people deviate from what people expect of them, their weaknesses dictate the extent of their growth.

Want to become an alcoholic? Here's one good way. Concentrate on your weaknesses and dwell upon every failure and mistake until you have consistent and gnawing feelings of guilt. Then, make sure you take *one* or *two* drinks each evening so you can "turn off" and go to sleep.

Soon, you will find *three* or *four* drinks work better. Soon, you will need *four* or *five* drinks. By this time, your guilt feelings will begin to change from *gnawing* to *consuming* doubts and you can become a real alcoholic in short order. Short prescription:

1. *Think only of yourself at all times*
2. *Concentrate on your weaknesses*

(Make negativism your creed)
3. *Seek relaxation by escape*
(Live passively)
4. *Stay away from church*

Perhaps the greatest sin a person can commit is to go through life constantly doubting himself and dwelling on his real or imagined inadequacies. Perhaps the greatest weakness in the worldwide fabric of space-age man is this befuddled and gutless tendency.

Building a Positive Personality

You have heard about the late, great chaplain of the United States Senate, Dr. Peter Marshall, who was one of the great ministers of our time.

Here are the headings for a number of the prayers of Peter Marshall:

> For More Faith
> For Newness of Life
> For Humility On the Mountain Top of Life
> For Consistency in the Christian Life
> For Childlikeness
> For One Burdened With Worry
> For Release From Tension
> For Release From Resentment
> For More Love
> For Our Family
> For Our Young People
> To Change The Spiritual Climate of the World
> For Liberation From Materialism
> For The Transforming of Everyday Life
> For Those In Pain
> For The Lonely
> For A Friend With A New Grief [2]

---

[2] Catharine Marshall, *The Prayers of Peter Marshall* (McGraw-Hill Book Co., Inc.).

I am sure most readers know that this great, bubbling energetic and ebullient man left an indelible imprint on our time. He was a man who spent practically no time expending vital energy, vital time, vital power on negatives. Here was an all-out quest for additional insight, additional faith, so that he could move solidly *for* the improvement, expansion, enrichment and overall progress of all of those for whom his words might have meaning. This was a man who truly built a positive personality. I commend his practices and a thorough reading of his biography to you as key blocks in the foundation of a positive personality.

The Theory of Crutches

You can plan an elaborate set of rationalizations or excuses for failure to achieve vigorous and meaningful actions every day of your life if you choose. They are all around us. You can always say, "I am too young" or "I am too old;" "I am too fat" or "I am too skinny;" "I have too much energy" or "I haven't enough energy;" "I have too much education" or "I do not have enough education."

It's ironic that we can find these crutches with great ease and we find it much more difficult to get rid of them because they seep in like slow poisons into our tissues, into our minds and we can slowly begin to succumb to their narcotic influences so that we even become proud of the fact that we are average, adequate, standard, ordinary, common—you name it—anything that smacks of comfortable, middle-classed, don't rock the boat, bland, meaninglessness and we can find a handy crutch to use to justify what we are *not* getting done.

I wonder if you know that you can actually sicken and die quickly from hate and worry alone. There are instances on record of people who have died within weeks of what was originally thought to be heartbreak. Additional information has disclosed that the person that felt a great hate towards some person who was still living following the loss of a loved one, or a sick and traumatic belief that God is an avenging God rather than a loving

God, the resentment and hate would well up, spoil the appetite, spoil the digestion, foul the breath, fog the eyes, dim the cheeks, of some of the strongest and most healthy people who succumb to the crutch called "hate." Hate can literally kill.

Probably, never before in the history of the world has the "health" industry been in such a state of prosperity. Almost everyone is interested in the latest pill, the newest tranquilizer, the newest fad diet, the newest mechanical vibrator that promises the easy way to health, and yet the most powerful, single ingredient for serene, but dynamic, quiet but surging health, lies right within each and every one of us. This is purely and simply the power to completely root out and displace every segment of hate with the most powerful, pure and effective emotions of all—*love*.

Do you have the courage? Do you have the self-discipline? to rigorously, ruthlessly, tenaciously root out every single segment of hate, cynicism, and defensiveness and replace it with love, faith and positivism.

Identification of Personal Challenges

Set at least one goal for every week of the next fifty-two weeks. Set a major annual goal for every year of the next ten years. It is essential that we all have goals, purposes and direction in order to keep self-preoccupation from building. We must have goals that *pull us out of ourselves.* We must create a climate which forces us to project, to keep our attentions going onward, to keep them focused upon goals, objectives, results which cannot be achieved in any way by self-preoccupation or concentration upon what we might want to get. We must concentrate instead on what we need to *give* to achieve a whole set of these personal challenges.

Measure whether our goals have sufficient challenge—look at our mistakes. If we don't make mistakes we are setting goals of insufficient challenge for mistakes need not be failures but lessons in our total growth process.

There is a natural desire to set comfortable goals, but when this is done, zest in living and passion for accomplishment is lost.

Why be comfortable when the healthy aged and the mentally alert old timers are evidence enough in the practicality of passionate living and challenging goals?

Don't Run From Success

This is an orderly, systematic and harmonious world in which we live in all ways, in all aspects, with regard to all elements—except the human element, the particular living creatures who have souls and who have conscious, reasoning minds. And we plunge onward and downward in search of what we finally imagine success to be through an all-out focus simply upon more money, more to eat, more to drink, more sex, more play, when, in precise reality, we are purely and simply running from total success as total people with the uncertain, compulsive, preoccupation with things which we can put down our gullet or experience with the extremities of our body. *Total success will always elude the person who seeks to achieve it on a purely material plan.* True success, true peace of mind, true development, must always lie and always will exist in the mind and in the spirit.

Many examples throughout history will show people who achieved much, who lived richly, who carved deep niches in history, who experienced very little in terms of money in the bank; but such people developed a tough quality of mind based upon a tall, growing, questing, spirited attitude, which was reflected in a mind preoccupied with outgoing results.

Steps for Accomplishment

Identify and define your own strengths.

1. List what you know about yourself, beginning with such characteristics as age, physical traits, interests, and stamina.

2. Develop a calculated schizophrenia—the ability to observe yourself in action.
3. Expose yourself to new and different situations.
4. Keep a written diary documenting your day-to-day observations. Periodically review it for recurrent patterns of behavior.
5. Find out what other people think of you and put their opinions in writing.
6. List your successes and extract the major contributing factors. As you concentrate on these successes, any failures should become insignificant.

Every man is valued in this world as he shows by his conduct that he wishes to be valued.

BRUYÉRE

14 "Un" Common as an Old Shoe

TO BE-OR NOT TO BE-UNCOMMON

Neighbors said Henry Jones was as "common as an old shoe." Even though Henry was mayor, he was always ready to help a neighbor out who was in need. Henry got his college degree after nearly ten years of going to school at nights after work.

He worked as a salesman for years—always one of the top for his company. He believed in his company, its products and himself. Henry organized and led the new building program for his church, and spearheaded the slum clearance movement within the community.

When graft was suspected in City Hall, Henry was asked to run for mayor on a reform platform. He ran and was elected.

They said he was "common" because he was considerate, gracious and sincere in dealing with people. These in themselves are pretty uncommon traits, and as you look at the whole picture I think you will agree that Henry was a pretty uncommon person.

Had he resorted to comfortableness he would have been common, but he took the uncomfortable road and became uncommon.

If you look at any dictionary definition of the word common we think you will find little satisfaction in commonness. Most definitions include statements such as "not gracious, vulgar, lacking of refinement, common in usage, second best, etc."

(Un) Common Courage

The person who complains much, who strikes out and bullies others, who constantly exhibits the turned-down mouth, the hate-filled eyes, the sardonic or savage reflections on the weaknesses and inadequacies of others should not be an object for fear, ridicule or contempt; but only an object for pity. Because this man is missing much that is great in life and the principal thing that he lacks is, obviously, courage. Because it takes courage to initially generate and feel faith in an age which seems too passive. It takes courage to search out and accumulate and weld together the values that we are discussing throughout this book. What is courage?

Courage is one of the supreme virtues known to man. Plato considered courage to be an element of the soul which bridges the cleavage between reason and desire. Aristotle thought of courage as the affirmation of man's essential nature. Thomas Aquinas said that "courage is a strength of mind capable of conquering whatever threatens the attainment of the highest good." "Courage," according to Dr. Martin Luther King, "is power of the mind to overcome fear."

Unlike anxiety, fear is a definite object which may be faced, analyzed, attacked and, if need be, endured. How often the object of our fear is fear itself. Henry David Thoreau said, "Nothing is so much to be feared, as fear." Epictetus wrote, "For it is not death or hardship that is a fearful thing, but the fear of hardship and death." Paul Tillich said, "Courage is self-affirmation 'in spite of' that which tends to hinder the self from affirming itself." To quote Martin Luther King again, "Courage, the determination not to be overwhelmed by any object however frightful—enables us to stand up to any fear." What a deep and meaningful description of that rare quality of tough-mindedness which makes a man truly uncommon.

In his famous classic, *The Power of Positive Thinking* (Prentice-Hall, Inc.), Norman Vincent Peale says, "Another profoundly curative element in the prescription for heartache is to gain a sound and satisfying philosophy of life, death and deathlessness. For my part, when I gained the unshakable belief that there is no death, that all life is indivisible, that the here and hereafter are one, that time and eternity are inseparable and that it is one unobstructed universe; then I found the most satisfying and convincing philosophy of my entire life."

Never say, "I am just a common man, or, I am just a common woman." There should be little time and patience for the person who leans upon the comfortable crutch of "commonness."

After you have carried out the process of extracting from the entire New Testament every sentence that uses the word "faith," and after you have underlined faith and memorized all of these sentences to the extent that you can, until they have become a living, breathing part of your central life mainstream, repeat day after day, "I reaffirm my faith." The word reaffirmation is a positive and powerful word. Because this is not a denial, not a negation of faith, this is simply saying I re-strengthen, I re-recognize, I re-integrate, and use and understand an abiding and enriching faith. Faith in country, faith in God and faith in the essential goodness of people.

Wisdom and Logic

What is wisdom? Wisdom is a quality which must be developed to a substantial extent in the fiery furnace of experience—although quite a number of young men have it. Wisdom must include an understanding of and can even develop because of, certain basic facts that are true of all so-called normal people. These basic facts include the following:

1. People differ from one another.
2. People have a need for spiritual guidance and belief.
3. People will usually do the thing that promises benefit to them, but human judgment often errs in determining what actions will yield this result.
4. To savor life you must work hard toward real accomplishment. Unused iron becomes rusty—stagnant water becomes murky.
5. True happiness comes only through giving to others of knowledge, encouragement, guidance, constructive criticism, faith, and of some material things.
6. Over the long pull it is impossible to give away more than you receive.
7. Dignity is a way of life not a convenient facade.
8. Intelligence expressed within a framework of self-interest alone is almost always futile when the end of the story is reached.
9. Untapped potential lies dormant in just about everyone.
10. Sacrificing individual liberty for collective security "never has produced real happiness."
11. Self-interest is normal and natural but can be truly realized only through and by the development of others.
12. We all have strengths and weaknesses but concentration in increasing the strengths will usually correct the weaknesses.
13. Education is not a destination but a continuing journey.

In summary, the person with wisdom *must* have values. He must have his own ideas, workable within the mores of our culture and the world, of what constitutes good and bad, sorrow and joy, moderation and intemperance. He must have appetites, but they must be directed toward positive achievement and must be controlled.

Put under each of the foregoing thirteen statements the following words: When, Where, Why, How—and then set out to develop answers to the when, where, how and why of each of these thirteen major pieces of fiber in the total carpet of wise tough-minded living and you will find this a meaningful and helpful system of constructive action.

In looking for a system of values which will meet our daily needs in helping us to prepare a concise and meaningful checklist for daily effectiveness in our jobs, take these thirteen steps. Take a close look and notice the indivisibility, of these statements. You will see that every single statement contains elements which touch upon every other statement in this list of thirteen. Study it carefully. Take each statement apart and look at its anatomy. Ask yourself if you're doing it now, if you're doing it well, if you're doing it as well as you can.

Ask other people for opinions on such things as the statement, "over the long pull it is impossible to give away more than you receive." Is this just a trite truism? A pliant platitude? A clodlike cliche? Or, do you have the courage to really give this a try—an all-out try? I would like to feel that those of you who have experimented and applied yourself with real diligence to the entire system of values described in this book will have discovered for yourself by now that it is indeed impossible to give away more than you receive; that the secret of power and success in this world of ours never lies in complexities but in simplicities; never in deviousness, but in straightforwardness; never in the circuitous way, but in the direct, pointed, targeted and focused way.

The word system, by its very nature, is pervasive and all encompassing. So, make a continuous effort to constantly weld together, meld together and completely unify all the principles in this book. It can seem from time to time as though there are an impossible number of basic truths and practices to master, but you will find that many of them are stating the same basic truth in a different way. This insures that all kinds of people with differing levels of maturity are all able to assimilate each of these truths in a way that is most meaningful to him. This, of course, is done in order to illustrate the thirteenth point in the description of the components of wisdom which is labeled "education is not a destination, but a continuing journey." And, if we truly apply this concept from this point till the day we die, we will indeed do much to insure that we knit together a whole set of procedures into a total system of interlaced values which continue to merge and build each other into a dynamic, total person.

Always keep in mind that all of life is governed by mighty, and only partially understood laws and principles, and that some of us are privileged enough in this lifetime to discover a great many more than others. And, if we are, this only increases the obligation to turn around and show our gratitude for this by giving freely to others of encouragement, of warmth, of empathy, of dignity, of direction and occasional shots of spiritual adrenalin.

Phonies Finish Last

"I remember one guy in particular who is now executive vice president of a big company, and he climbed up there right over the bleeding backs of everybody who got in his way—he was a phony in every sense of the word. He was a downright crook. He engaged in office politics, he cut and he slashed and he's up there. You can't tell me that this guy finished last." Or another person might point out, "What about so-and-so? When I see him drive down the street in that big Cadillac of his and an expensive fat stogie stuck in his face, I hate that guy because I know he's been a phony all of his life. Everybody hates him—you can't tell me that this guy has finished last."

This particular executive vice president may still be Executive Vice President—maybe he has even become president, but he is still building on sand. If he has sacrificed his integrity and engaged in poisonous political manipulations over the years, he might even still be in the job when he retires; but time and time again I have seen men climb right up to the vice presidential level and all of a sudden they drop quietly out of the corporate ranks because an investigation will reveal that the whole legacy of untruths began to catch up with them, the noose descends, the blade of the guillotine drops and he is on the outside looking in. And, I have seen the careers of some of these men in their forties and sixties when they should be in full bloom, begin a disastrous plunge that takes many of them almost to the depths so that they have gone into retirement or died in virtual and literal disgrace.

Then, too, let's take the millionaire who dies and leaves a million dollars in the bank. You say this man has "not finished last" because he had a million dollars right up to the day he died. All right—try this on for size. If he dies and leaves behind him no legacy of love, and no legacy of respect, then any way you slice it —this man has finished last. All he left behind him was a pile of paper in the bank and this is absolutely no comparison; it cannot hold a candle to the legacy of people who revere his memory with love, respect and warm and savory memories. I repeat—with absolutely no apology, no qualification or equivocation—a phony will *always* finish last! !

The Grand Design

Recently we conducted a series of development sessions at Estes Park, Colorado. The volatile and dynamic changes which took place in this group during the five-day conference are worth noting here.

On Monday morning the Conference Room filled with a group of men who had just become acquainted for the first time. We went around the room asking each executive, government official and scientist why he was there, what he hoped to achieve and what his principal problems and objectives were. The answers were adequate, they were status quo and stereotyped.

"I want to increase the profit of my company."
"I want to learn more about communications."
"I want to know how to motivate people."
"I want to reduce costs and waste."

As the session unfolded, heavy stress was placed on the *philosophy* or *grand design* of each man. A total of two days was devoted to working out and clarifying the personal values of each. It became clear that the reasons given for being there were only superficial. Each man really wanted peace of mind, abundant health, revitalized confidence, energy, staying power, productivity and spiritual power.

Here are some of the assignments they were given:

1. Stand up and state what is the phoniest thing about you, and what you are going to *do* about it.

2. What is it you fear most, and what are you going to *do* about it.

3. Study "Tough-Minded Management" during the evenings with your wife and be prepared to state what you are *for* as a man by Friday. And—what you are going to *do* about it.

4. List ten things you would *do* if you suddenly became president of your organization next Monday. (Or, if you are now the top executive, name ten things you would *do* if you became President of the United States.)

5. List your five greatest strengths—and what you are going to *do* about them.

The difference between Monday and Friday was gratifying indeed. At the end of the week each man had moved forward, at first gropingly, toward an examination and understanding of his *real* needs, *real* desires, *real* problems, *real* source of strength and inspiration. The reader who is unschooled in management will not care particularly about the major tools discussed such as Management Information Systems, Corporate Planning, Profit Teams and the like. But—it is important for all readers to understand that the best and most efficient use of plant and office facilities, equipment and machinery, bank balances and systems and procedures are *only* possible through, by and for *people*. And people are only as effective as the strength of their *minds*, and their minds are only as strong as the *beliefs* and *values* which nourish them.

A rocket scientist said, "I came here an avowed atheist—I'm going to change." The new sparkle in his eyes supported his statement. The youngest man in the entire group commented on "—

this crazy country where virtually all people need and want new spiritual power and energy—and yet, few of them can even mention God or Jesus at a social gathering without lowering their voices and looking almost furtive." (Furtive?) Yes! An amazing number of "hardshelled" executives and professional men look relieved indeed when they discover the listener wants to hear more. (And they most always do!) How silly can we get?

For example, a group called "Full Gospel Businessmen's Voice" was established just a few years ago with headquarters in Los Angeles and as soon as thousands of businessmen heard that conventions would be held simply to discuss abundant, dedicated and healthful living in close consonance with the hundreds of promises in the Bible, their ranks swelled from dozens to hundreds to thousands and now have chapters forming in remote corners of the world.

When the basic beliefs of Moral Re-armament (described by Peter Howard in "Design for Dedication") were laid before influential business and professional groups, the membership swelled by the thousands and is now world-wide and poses as one of the most major deterrents to the poisonous spread of Communism. Its ideology? *Christianity*—pure and simple!!

And so-called normal people want—indeed *must* have—something greater than themselves to live, work and passionately strive for. The hard-nosed general manager of a large chemical plant who attended the conference said, "What I have learned in the past five days will change my life profoundly. I wondered at first the other morning why on earth an expert on tough-mindedness was talking about things like love, compassion, Americanism and so on. As I got involved in the whole thing my whole conception of my job shifted around, doubts and uncertainty left me and I can hardly wait to get back to the job. Incidentally, I was impressed with that word, Spiritual Engineering. I was able to virtually whip out my slide rule and begin to chart a set of spiritual goals, timetables and controls."

These men were well on their way, at the end of five days, to becoming uncommon men.

The Grand Design—In Practice

The bread and butter proof of what developing purpose, philosophy and a design to life can do can be well demonstrated by the story of Berkley Bedell.

In 1964, Berkley Bedell, President of the Berkley Company, was presented a National Award by the President of the United States as "Small Businessman of the Year."

Starting his business as a high school boy in his basement he has progressed to a modern factory distributing products throughout the world. Along the way Berk Bedell worked out his personal objectives and philosophies. They have contributed tremendously to his success. His beliefs have conditioned and saturated every major policy, procedure and decision.

Here are the personal objectives of Berkley Bedell, the nation's outstanding small businessman in 1964.

A. *To have a good time, and bring fun, happiness, and joy to others.*

Methods of accomplishing this will include the following:

1. Try to make fun out of whatever I am doing.
2. Be enthusiastic about all my tasks.
3. Develop as wide a range of interests as possible, and guard against getting in a rut in recreational activities and interests.
4. Include others in my recreational activities whenever possible, particularly others who might not otherwise get to enjoy the activity. Examples would include taking children, employees, relatives, and friends fishing, camping, travelling and the like.
5. Share my recreational facilities with others. This would include ice skating rink, tennis court, boats, beach, dock, etc.
6. Have a complete physical at least once each year, so that I may know how actively I may engage in athletic sports without danger to my health.

7. Always place fun ahead of winning in competitive contests.
8. Try to always be cheerful and wear a smile regardless of the problems.
9. Do an average of at least one deed a day which will bring happiness to someone. Keep a diary as a scorecard to be sure that this is kept up.
10. Try to be understanding of others whose views may differ from mine.
11. Try to keep engaged in work which I enjoy.

B. *To raise a well-adjusted family, helping them develop so that they will live happy lives, and contribute toward making the world a better place in which to live.*

Methods of accomplishing this will include the following:

1. Always set a good example for my family by being honest, ambitious, conscientious, friendly, humble, and fun.
2. Encourage them in whatever they want to do, and have confidence in their abilities.
3. Spend time having fun with my family even when business matters are pressing, or I do not have the ambition for play.
4. Administer discipline when necessary, but try to teach them so that they need a minimum of discipline.
5. Take an active interest in their activities.
6. Take an active interest in, and participate in, community youth activities such as school, scouts, etc.
7. Attend church and Sunday School together.
8. Pray together.
9. Teach my family to work.
10. Encourage my family to get a good education, and provide them with the necessary financial assistance to enable them to get a college education.
11. Direct my recreational activities toward family activities as much as possible, including family travel, picnics, fishing, hunting, swimming, skating, boating and the like.
12. Show them as much of the world as possible, so as to

broaden their knowledge and help them plan their future lives.

C. *To live in such a manner as to cause the world to be a little better place to live because of my having been here.*

Methods of accomplishing this will include the following:

1. Try to live in such a manner as to set a good example for others.
2. Use the profits of my labor to try to bring about community and social improvements, and to help others.
3. Spend at least 10% of my income each year for the church and charitable projects.
4. Try to lead others into giving more of their wealth and time for charity and worthwhile projects.
5. Share the profits of my plants with my fellow employees, and encourage them to be good citizens.
6. Try to see that the youth of my community, and any community wherein I locate a plant are not denied a college education because of lack of money.
7. Try to direct my hours of labor so that I may be of the most service in trying to accomplish this objective. These hours should be divided between the management of my business ventures, service in public office, or work in charitable or service projects as the need appears, and my contribution would be the greatest.
8. Be not afraid to speak out for or work for that which I feel is right, but always give consideration to the thoughts and feelings of other, and realize that reform and improvement does not always come as fast as I might like.
9. Try to preserve my health, as the amount of service I can render is dependent upon my health.
10. Work for self improvement through study, and attendance at schools, seminars and the like, so that I may be of more value to my company and mankind.

There is no stopping people like Mr. Bedell who have worked out a purpose in life. Berk's company has been one of our most cherished clients. We are proud indeed!

The Tap Roots of Warmth

One of the most brilliant young businessmen that I have ever observed seriously hampered his career for a number of years because he had not yet learned what will be discussed in this section.

To the men that worked with him, there were no doubts about his brilliance. He had high intelligence, very alert, well educated and informed on many subjects. Yet—he lacked wisdom and warmth. In the office he was the clown and when starring in his office arena his barbed humor hurt and offended many co-workers. A weekend basketball game with other executives found him making most of the baskets while the older men with less speed and stamina got little chance to participate.

In meetings he showed little consideration for his colleagues as he demonstrated his keen mind and exceptional verbal ability many times dominating the sessions with his persuasive gymnastics. He had to prove to himself that he was a man—and as a result he acted like a boy!!

Frequently the company executive vice president would talk with him pointing out how he had failed time and again to show consideration for the feelings of others and was developing the image of "self-centered jackass." Religiously, for a few weeks after these sessions, he would begin to develop the little courtesies dictated by Emily Post, but this insincerity came to the forefront when he would relax his superficial effort to be "nice."

One of the executives was off work for several days as a result of a severe bruising when rammed into a tree by this young man in a touch football game. The executive vice president firmly laid down the law—he had six months to grow up and become a man, or in spite of his abilities he would no longer be employed by the firm.

"What in the world are you trying to prove?" he asked him. "What are you afraid of?" At first he would not admit to being afraid of anything, but suddenly he quit bluffing and admitted to many fears. Fears that to overcome he had to keep proving to others how capable he was both mentally and physically.

His superior asked him:

"Is charging so hard, in a game of play, that someone is injured —is this the behavior of a man?"

"Is playing the cynic and the buffoon—is this the behavior of a man?"

"Is displaying your intelligence and verbal ability to the point that others who have good ideas cannot even participate in the discussion—is this the behavior of a man?"

"Is being the star and stealing the limelight when you're in athletic activities with men of lesser prowess than you—is this the behavior of a man?"

"Is having secretaries cry over hurt from your remarks and your lack of consideration—is this the behavior of a man?"

They agreed that this type of behavior was not that of a mature man, but that of an adolescent.

The executive vice president recommended that for the next six months he concentrate only on being as effective as possible on his job. He should not try to prove anything to anybody regarding his capabilities during this same period, but let his deeds speak for themselves. Coupled with this, to try and manifest graciousness and warmth.

Once this young man got over trying to prove to everyone else how good he was—he was able to begin to develop a sincere interest in others making it possible for him to become a much warmer, consequently more effective, individual.

Real warmth and graciousness cannot be developed as long as one is concerned primarily with self-image.

American businessmen are criticized for lacking graciousness, probably more than any group of businessmen in the world.

In Europe, our executives are accused of being all business and having no time for the normal pleasantries of social interchange and often are not the least bit concerned with the local country's customs and conventions. The old truism of "When in Rome do as the Romans do" has to be considered to some extent by the businessman who wants to be thought of as a warm and considerate person, when abroad. There is no doubt that American business has suffered economically from the "Ugly American" image.

For the American businessman who does go abroad, much can be learned in the practices of grace by studying his foreign counterpart.

Remember! There is nothing tough-minded or masculine about having an image of being a bull in a chinaware shop.

An individual whom I greatly respect once told me an excellent measurement for how warm and gracious a person is: how well they can give and receive a compliment. The gracious person can accept the compliment as well as give one.

The uncommon person is gracious and warm.

The Busy Man Is the Happy Man

The old phrase, "If you want something done, give it to a busy man" has always been true and I suppose it always will be true. Hence the busy man does not have time to meditate on why he cannot get a thing done and how fate may fail to smile upon him, or to visualize in detail all of the roadblocks or pitfalls that may get in his way. He is accustomed to bouncing out of bed in the morning with his mind focused on what he's got to get done, instead of how poorly he feels. He is thinking about that business engagement or that professional call or the particular chores of the day, and he looks in the mirror and shaves, rather than inspecting his tongue to see if it is coated, rather than looking at his eyes to see if they are bleary.

This man simply doesn't have the time to fail, he simply doesn't have the time to give himself reasons and more reasons for not getting a thing done. Thus he *"gets* it done."

You, too, can be that kind of a man or woman. The only person who can stand in the way of this kind of vibrant, radiant, day-to-day accomplishment is you.

The Snowy Heights of Honor

Longfellow wrote: The heights by great men reached and kept were not attained by sudden flight but they, while their companions slept, were turning upward in the night."

Ralph Waldo Emerson has said, "If a man can write a better book, preach a better sermon, or make a better mousetrap than his neighbor, though he build his house in the woods, the world will make a beaten path to his door."

And from Martin Luther King's book, *Strength To Love* (Harper, 1963) here are examples of people who have aspired to the heights:

> From an old slave cabin in Virginia's hills Booker T. Washington rose to become one of America's great leaders. From the oppressive red hills of Gordon County, Georgia, and the arms of a mother who could neither read nor write, Roland Hayes emerged as one of the world's most foremost singers. His melodious voice was heard in the palaces of kings and the mansions of queens. Coming from a poverty-stricken environment in Philadelphia, Marian Anderson achieved the distinction of being the world's greatest contralto, so much so that Toscanini said "A voice like hers comes only once in a century" and Sibelius explained that his roof was too low for such a voice.
>
> From crippling circumstance, George Washington Carver made for himself an imperishable niche in the annals of science.
>
> Ralph J. Bunche, the grandson of a slave preacher, has brought a rare distinction to diplomacy. These are only a few of the numerous examples that remind us that in spite of our lack for freedom we can make a contribution here and now.
>
> We are challenged on every hand to work untiringly to achieve excellence in our life work.

Regardless of your color, race or creed, it must be manifest that any of the noted Negroes cited in Dr. King's book faced infinitely greater handicaps than many of the people reading this book. But these were people who developed that rare quality of mind which we have termed "toughness," and which has much in common with a tender heart. They had a strong drive for self-fulfillment. In the case of Miss Anderson, for instance, this self-fulfillment was achieved so magnificently because of her all-out dedicated and disciplined quest for excellence in giving, for excellence in providing for listeners throughout the world a rare quality of esthetic joy and exultation in hearing the beautiful instrument that her disciplined and dedicated voice has become.

Thrill to the phrase, "The snowy heights of honor." There is room for every man whether he is Chinese, Japanese, Korean, Negro; whether he be Caucasoid, Mongoloid—whatever he may be. There is room for high goals. There is a crying need for giants, even though they may not exceed five feet in height, who push toward, who labor toward, who never take their eyes off the snowy heights of honor which are represented by man's inherent knowledge when he lies in the dark at night or when he looks in the mirror—that he be given to the enrichment of other men; that he help to contribute to the delineation, the shaping up and the expression of other people's integrity. He recognizes that the requirements for the Sermon on the Mount are not idle phrases to toss about in the after-dinner circuit or in the hot-stove league or in far out philosophical discussions. He knows that the requirements of the Sermon on the Mount constitute the finest possible pinnacles in man's experience. They constitute, in reality, nothing less than snowy heights of honor and he thrills to a sense of mission. He feels that it is not corny. It is pleasant, it is zestful, it is stimulating, it is stretching, it is pulse-quickening to clarify the mission; to focus on the heights, to define and build the steps to the application of what, where, when, who, how and why, to the understanding of how to plan, organize, direct, coordinate and control the daily practices and daily expenditures of energy. And that the rest of his life will be spent in a persistent, steady ascent step by step toward the snowy heights of achievement which we have called the snowy height of honor. Repeat, talk about, think about and write about the snowy heights of honor.

Up there the atmosphere is clear; up there there is regrettably an extremely small, but very select group of tall individuals who walk straight with purpose, who judge men by their basic dignity and their deeds rather than by their color, race or creed, and who thrill to the mission of giving, building, striving and expanding.

My life shall touch a dozen lives
  Before this day is done,
Leave countless marks of good or ill,
  Ere sets the evening sun.
This, the wish I always wish,
  The prayer I always pray:
Lord, may my life help other lives
  It touches by the way.

ANONYMOUS

15 No Man Is an Island

NO MAN IS AN ISLAND

No man is an island. A famous biologist spent twenty years studying cells and micro-organisms under a microscope and he came to one basic conclusion—life needs organization and cooperative effort even in such things as cells. If one little cell scoots off from the rest and tries to live alone in a limbo, it soon shrivels up and calls it a day. The same is true of human beings. No man is an island —we're all bound together.

Many people today think that they are self-sufficient, that they can get along without being integrated into the society of mankind. Our country was built by the cooperative effort of our pioneers who had their house-raisings, depended on each other for protection and showed constant willingness to serve each other.

As we become more metropolitan we feel we can be more independent, but the truth is that in a crisis we are more dependent than ever on each other. The late Doctor Tom Dooley in his book, *The Night They Burned the Mountain* (Farrar, Straus & Giroux, Inc.), said: "The only reason for your existence is not what you're going to get out of life, but what you are going to put into it." What you give of yourself in this great community of man, is your primary reason for existence.

In the book "Tough-Minded Management" it says: "True happiness comes only through giving to others—of knowledge, of encouragement, of guidance, of constructive criticism, of faith, of some material things—and over the long pull it is impossible to give away more than you receive." The long pull, can of course, include the hereafter.

Arlene Francis, of the "What's My Line?" panel, in her book on charm—*That Certain Something* (Julian Messner, Inc.) says, "I think genuine charm is an unmotivated interest in others."

Psychologists and psychiatrists have found that those who try to give more to life in service than they expect in return are the happiest. That those that are worried that someone is going to take advantage of them and live in a world of self-concern are the ones that are neurotic, live in fear, and are basically unhappy. It appears that one of the most unforgivable things regarding "the little person" is their inability to forgive. True grace requires not only the ability to give thanks and apology, but being able to receive this from others. Being able to forgive is a part of building on strengths, not focusing on weaknesses. Continued character assassination is going on in this world. There is often a kind of constant erosion of people because we focus on their weaknesses, their shortcomings, their failures—and overlook their strengths and their accomplishments. It seems sometimes that Jesus' saying in the book of Matthew "Judge not, that ye be not judged" is a most violated scripture. The gratification, the intangible compensation of a minister we have met, who has spent his life running a mission near Chicago's skid row, is hard for us to estimate. This man has rehabilitated many former convicts, alcoholics, and all types of failures. Among the former derelicts that he has given much of his life to are a number who have since become internationally known, in their respective fields.

Had this minister of the gospel only seen their weaknesses and failures—had he not looked for their strengths, prayed for them, helped them develop faith in God—faith in mankind—and faith in self much could have been lost for all mankind.

We will be judged by what we have done, by the love we have shown. Can we hide behind the excuse of fatigue or weariness? No! Not if we really understand that the principal cause of tiredness in the average person is a weariness with self. *You need something better than yourself to live for!!*

How can we not care about giving of ourself, when we look around us and see such great need. Our service can not be communicated from the sidelines—we must commit ourselves and become involved with others.

We have all known people who have had a great deal of self-confidence and faith in themselves—and others that have had very little of this. Careful observation should show you that those people that have a true self-confidence, not only have a faith in themselves, but they have faith in mankind and a faith in an Almighty. The ebullient, totally happy person that is passionately pursuing positive goals in life must not be concerned with getting, but of giving of self. Tom Dooley also said in his book, "are you willing to ignore what the world owes you and think of what you owe the world—to put your rights in the background, your duties in the middle ground, and your chances to do—more than your duty in the foreground?" It is "your chances to do" that makes the difference between success and mediocrity.

In the beginning we urged you to arm yourself with a *positive philosophy,* gird yourself with *positive principles,* and sustain this philosophy, these principles and these practices with faith, and live this faith with passion. To resolve to live life to its fullest. To walk tall with sure knowledge that the world needs, and is hungry for, **the big, tough-minded individual.**

Peter Howard in his excellent book—*Design for Dedication* (Henry Regnery Co., Chicago) says:

"You fight the Communists economically. You fight them politically. You fight them militantly if you must. But where is the common ideology shared by all free men which says to the Communist world: 'You are out of date; you are outmoded. We are going to put this world right far quicker than you can do it?'" *We hope you have found in these pages the fiber and fabric for such an ideology. We hope you will exemplify it throughout the world.*

So, in summary, look to the future, don't look back. Stay *un*satisfied, but not *dis*satisfied. Look for grimness and bleakness in life and you will find it. Look for abundance and joy—for productivity and success—and you will find them.

Dare to get out of yourself and live a passionate life.

Don't live a little—live a lot!

We challenge you to become the *ultimate you!*

AUTHOR'S NOTE

Dare to read, soak up and *master* the four appendices which follow:

    APPENDIX 1   THE TEN COMMANDMENTS
    APPENDIX 2   THE SERMON ON THE MOUNT
    APPENDIX 3   THE UNITED STATES CONSTITUTION
    APPENDIX 4   DESIGN FOR WORLD HARMONY THROUGH LAW AND EXAMPLE.

We think you will be amazed and delighted to discover the functional, compatible operational blending of these great manifestoes. Every single statement has significance for you as you step up your pace in confronting and savoring life's challenges.

You will find them to be wellsprings of spiritual, social, economic and legal power—may they gush forth torrents of inspiration, strength, honor and unity for you and yours. Cemented securely by the mortar of passionate living, you will find the ingredients for an ideology which can truly make the world a better place in which to live.

APPENDIX 1

THE TEN COMMANDMENTS

THOU SHALT HAVE NO OTHER GODS BEFORE ME.

THOU SHALT NOT TAKE THE NAME OF THE LORD THY GOD IN VAIN; FOR THE LORD WILL NOT HOLD HIM GUILTLESS THAT TAKETH HIS NAME IN VAIN.

REMEMBER THE SABBATH DAY, TO KEEP IT HOLY.

HONOR THY FATHER AND THY MOTHER, THAT THY DAYS MAY BE LONG UPON THE LAND WHICH THE LORD THY GOD GIVETH THEE.

THOU SHALT NOT KILL.

THOU SHALT NOT COMMIT ADULTERY.

THOU SHALT NOT STEAL.

THOU SHALT NOT BEAR FALSE WITNESS AGAINST THY NEIGHBOR.

THOU SHALT NOT COVET THY NEIGHBOR'S HOUSE.

THOU SHALT NOT COVET THY NEIGHBOR'S WIFE, NOR HIS MANSERVANT, NOR HIS MAIDSERVANT, NOR HIS CATTLE, NOR ANYTHING THAT IS THY NEIGHBOR'S.

APPENDIX 2

THE SERMON ON THE MOUNT
Phillips Modern English Version

Jesus proclaims the new values of the kingdom:

When Jesus saw the vast crowds he went up the hillside, and after he had sat down his disciples came to him.

Then he began his teaching by saying to them:

"How happy are the humble-minded, for the kingdom of Heaven is theirs!

"How happy are those who know what sorrow means, for they will be given courage and comfort!

"Happy are those who claim nothing, for the whole earth will belong to them!

"Happy are those who are hungry and thirsty for goodness, for they will be fully satisfied!

"Happy are the merciful, for they will have mercy shown to them.

"Happy are the utterly sincere, for they will see God!

"Happy are those who make peace, for they will be known as sons of God!

"Happy are those who have suffered persecution for the cause of goodness, for the kingdom of Heaven is theirs!

"And what happiness will be yours when people blame you and ill-treat you and say all kinds of slanderous things against you for my sake! Be glad then, yes, be tremendously glad—for your reward in Heaven is magnificent. They persecuted the prophets before your time in exactly the same way.

"You are the earth's salt. But if the salt should become tasteless, what can make it salt again? It is completely useless and can only be thrown out of doors and stamped underfoot.

"You are the world's light—it is impossible to hide a town built on the top of a hill. Men do not light a lamp and put it under a bucket.

They put it on a lampstand, and it gives light for everybody in the house.

"Let your light shine like that in the sight of men. Let them see the good things you do and praise your Father in Heaven.

Christ's authority surpasses that of the Law:

"You must not think that I have come to abolish the Law or the Prophets; I have not come to abolish them but to complete them. Indeed, I assure you that, while Heaven and earth last, the Law will not lose a single dot or comma until its purpose is complete. This means that whoever now relaxes one of the least of these commandments and teaches men to do the same will himself be called least in the Kingdom of Heaven. For I tell you that your goodness must be a far better thing than the goodness of the scribes and Pharisees before you can set foot in the kingdom of Heaven at all!

"You have heard that it was said to the people in the old days, 'Thou shalt not murder,' and anyone who does so must stand his trial. But I say to you that anyone who is angry with his brother must stand his trial. But I say to you that anyone who is angry with his brother a fool must face the supreme court; and anyone who looks down on his brother as a lost soul is himself heading straight for the fire of destruction.

"So that if, while you are offering your gift at the altar, you should remember that your brother has something against you, you must leave your gift there before the altar and go away. Make your peace with your brother first, then come and offer your gift. Come to terms quickly with your opponent while you have the chance, or else he may hand you over to the judge and the judge in turn hand you over to the officer of the court and you will be thrown into prison. Believe me, you will never get out again till you have paid your last farthing!

"You have heard that it was said to the people in the old days, 'Thou shalt not commit adultery.' But I say to you that every man who looks at a woman lustfully has already committed adultery with her—in his heart.

"Yes, if your right eye leads you astray pluck it out and throw it away; it is better for you to lose one of your members than that your whole body should go to the rubbish heap.

"It also used to be said that whoever divorces his wife must give her a proper certificate of divorce. But I say to you that whoever divorces his wife except on the ground of unfaithfulness is making her an adulteress. And whoever marries the woman who has been divorced also commits adultery.

"Again, you have heard that the people in the old days were told—'Thou shalt not forswear thyself, but shalt perform unto the Lord thine oaths'; but I say to you, don't use an oath at all. Don't swear by Heaven for it is God's throne; nor by the earth for it is his footstool; not by Jerusalem for it is the city of the great king. No, and don't swear by your own head, for you cannot make a single hair—white or black! Whatever you have to say let your 'yes' be a plain 'yes' and your 'no' be a plain 'no'—anything more than this has a taint of evil.

"You have heard that it used to be said 'An eye for an eye and a tooth for a tooth,' but I tell you, don't resist the man who wants to harm you. If a man hits your right cheek, turn the other one to him as well. If a man wants to sue you for your coat, let him have it and your overcoat as well. If anybody forces you to go a mile with him, do more—go two miles with him. Give to the man who asks anything from you, and don't turn away from the man who wants to borrow.

"You have heard that it used to be said 'Thou shalt love thy neighbor and hate thine enemy,' but I tell you, Love your enemies, and pray for those who persecute you, so that you may be sons of your Heavenly Father. For he makes his sun rise upon evil men as well as good, and he sends his rain upon honest and dishonest men alike.

"For if you love only those who love you, what credit is that to you? Even tax collectors do that! And if you exchange greetings only with your own circle, are you doing anything exceptional? Even the pagans do that much. No, you are to be perfect, like your Heavenly Father.

The new life is not a matter of outward show:

"Beware of doing your good deeds conspicuously to catch men's eyes or you will miss the reward of your Heavenly Father.

"So, when you do good to other people, don't hire a trumpeter to go in front of you—like those play actors in the synagogues and streets who make sure that men admire them. Believe me, they have had all the reward they are going to get! No, when you give to charity, don't even let your left hand know what your right hand is doing, so that your giving may be secret. Your Father who knows all secrets will reward you.

"And then, when you pray, don't be like the play actors. They love to stand and pray in the synagogues and at street corners so that people may see them at it. Believe me, they have had all the reward they are going to get! But when you pray, go into your own room, shut your door and pray to your Father privately. Your Father who sees all private things will reward you. And when you pray don't rattle off long prayers like the pagans who think they will be heard because they use so many words. Don't be like them. After all, God, who is your Father, knows your needs before you ask him. Pray then like this—

Our Heavenly Father, may your name be honored;
May your kingdom come and your will be done on earth as it is in Heaven.
Give us this day the bread we need,
Forgive us what we owe to you, as we have also forgiven those who owe anything to us.
Keep us clear of temptation, and save us from evil.

Forgiveness of fellow man is essential:

"For if you forgive other people their failures, your Heavenly Father will also forgive you. But if you will not forgive other people, neither will your Heavenly Father forgive you your failures.

"Then, when you fast, don't look like those miserable play actors! For they deliberately disfigure their faces so that people may see that they are fasting. Believe me, they have had all their reward. No, when you fast brush your hair and wash your face so that nobody knows that you are fasting—let it be a secret between you and your Father. And your Father who knows all secrets will reward you.

Put your trust in God alone:

"Don't pile up treasures on earth, where moth and rust can spoil them and thieves can break in and steal. But keep your treasure in Heaven where there is neither moth nor rust to spoil it and nobody can break in and steal. For wherever your treasure is, you may be certain that your heart will be there too!

"The lamp of the body is the eye. If your eye is sound, your whole body will be full of light. But if your eye is evil, your whole body will be full of darkness. If all the light you have is darkness, it is dark indeed!

"No one can be loyal to two masters. He is bound to hate one and love the other, or support one and despise the other. You cannot serve God and the power of money at the same time. That is why I say to you, don't worry about living—wondering what you are going to eat or drink, or what you are going to wear. Surely life is more important than food, and the body more important than the clothes you wear. Look at the birds in the sky. They never sow nor reap nor store away in barns, and yet your Heavenly Father feeds them. Aren't you much more valuable to him than they are? Can any of you, however much he worries, make himself an inch taller? And why do you worry about clothes? Consider how the wild flowers grow. They neither work nor weave, but I tell you that even Solomon in all his glory was never arrayed like one of these! Now if God so clothes the flowers of the field, which are alive today and burned in the stove tomorrow, is he not much more likely to clothe you, you 'little-faiths'?

"So don't worry and don't keep saying, 'What shall we eat, what shall we drink or what shall we wear?' That is what pagans are always looking for; your Heavenly Father knows that you need them all. Set your heart on his kingdom and his goodness, and all these things will come to you as a matter of course.

"Don't worry at all then about tomorrow. Tomorrow can take care of itself! One day's trouble is enough for one day.

The common sense behind right behavior:

"Don't criticize people, and you will not be criticized. For you will be judged by the way you criticize others, and the measure you give will be the measure you receive.

"Why do you look at the speck of sawdust in your brother's eye and fail to notice the plank in your own? How can you say to your brother, 'Let me get the speck out of your eye,' when there is a plank in your own? You fraud! Take the plank out of your own eye first, and then you can see clearly enough to remove your brother's speck of dust.

"You must not give holy things to dogs, nor must you throw your pearls before pigs—or they may trample them underfoot and turn and attack you.

"Ask and it will be given to you. Search and you will find. Knock and the door will be opened for you. The one who asks will always receive; the one who is searching will always find, and the door is opened to the man who knocks.

"If any of you were asked by his son for bread would you be likely to give him a stone, or if he asks for a fish would you give him a snake? If you then, for all your evil, quite naturally give good things to your children, how much more likely is it that your Heavenly Father will give good things to those who ask him?

"Treat other people exactly as you would like to be treated by them —this is the essence of all true religion.

"Go in by the narrow gate. For the wide gate has a broad road which leads to disaster, and there are many people going that way. The narrow gate and the hard road lead out into life, and only a few are finding it.

Living, not professing, is what matters:

"Be on your guard against false religious teachers, who come to you dressed up as sheep but are really greedy wolves. You can tell them by their fruit. Do you pick a bunch of grapes from a thornbush or figs from a clump of thistles? Every good tree produces good fruit, and a bad tree cannot produce good fruit. The tree that fails to produce good fruit is cut down and burned. So you may know men by their fruit.

"It is not everyone who keeps saying to me 'Lord, Lord' who will enter the kingdom of Heaven, but the man who actually does my Heavenly Father's will.

"In 'that day' many will say to me, 'Lord, Lord, didn't we preach in your name, didn't we cast out devils in your name, and do many great things in your name?' Then I shall tell them plainly: 'I have never known you. Go away from me; you have worked on the side of evil!'

To follow Christ's teaching means the only real security:

"Everyone then who hears these words of mine and puts them into practice is like a sensible man who builds his house on the rock. Down came the rain and up came the floods, while the winds blew and roared upon that house—and it did not fall because its foundations were on rock.

"And everyone who hears these words of mine and does not follow them can be compared with a foolish man who built his house on the sand. Down came the rain and up came the floods, while the winds blew and battered that house till it collapsed, and fell with a great crash."

When Jesus had finished these words the crowd were astonished at the power behind his teaching. For his words had the ring of authority, quite unlike those of their scribes. (For further interpretation, you are urged to read *The Sermon on the Mount,* by Emmett Fox—Harper and Brothers.)

APPENDIX 3

THE UNITED STATES CONSTITUTION

PREAMBLE

We the people of the United States, in order to form a more perfect union, establish justice, insure domestic tranquility, provide for the common defense, promote the general welfare, and secure the blessings of liberty to ourselves and our posterity, do ordain and establish this Constitution for the United States of America.

ARTICLE I

THE LEGISLATIVE DEPARTMENT

Section 1. All legislative powers herein granted shall be vested in a Congress of the United States, which shall consist of a Senate and House of Representatives.

THE HOUSE OF REPRESENTATIVES

Section 2. (1) The House of Representatives shall be composed of members chosen every second year by the people of the several States, and the electors in each State shall have the qualifications requisite for electors of the most numerous branch of the State legislature.

(2) No person shall be a Representative who shall not have attained to the age of twenty-five years, and been seven years a citizen of the United States, and who shall not, when elected, be an inhabitant of that State in which he shall be chosen.

(3) Representatives and direct taxes shall be apportioned among the several States which may be included within this union, according to their respective numbers, (which shall be determined by adding to the whole number of free persons, including those bound to service for a term of years), and excluding Indians not taxed, (three-fifths of all other persons). The actual enumeration shall be made within three years after the first meeting of the Congress of the United States, and within every subsequent term of ten years, in such manner as they shall by law direct. The number of Representatives shall not exceed one for every thirty thousand, but each State shall have at least one representative; (and until such enumeration shall be made, the State of New Hampshire shall be entitled to choose 3, Massachusetts 8, Rhode Island and Providence Plantations 1, Connecticut 5, New York 6, New Jersey 4, Pennsylvania 8, Delaware 1, Maryland 6, Virginia 10, North Carolina 5, South Carolina 5, and Georgia 3).

(4) When vacancies happen in the representation from any State, the executive authority thereof shall issue writs of election to fill such vacancies.

(5) The House of Representatives shall choose their Speaker and other officers; and shall have the sole power of impeachment.

THE UNITED STATES SENATE

Section 3. (1) The Senate of the United States shall be composed of two Senators from each State, (chosen by the legislature thereof,) for six years; and each Senator shall have one vote.

(2) Immediately after they shall be assembled in consequence of the first election, they shall be divided as equally as may be into three classes. The seats of the senators of the first class shall be vacated at the expiration of the second year, of the second class at the expiration of the fourth year, and of the third class at the expiration of the sixth year, so that one third may be chosen every second year; (and if vacancies happen by resignation, or otherwise, during the recess of the legislature of any State, the Executive thereof may make temporary appointments until the next meeting of the legislature, which shall then fill such vacancies).

(3) No person shall be a Senator who shall not have attained to the age of thirty years, and been nine years a citizen of the

United States, and who shall not, when elected, be an inhabitant of that State for which he shall be chosen.

(4) The Vice-President of the United States shall be President of the Senate, but shall have no vote, unless they be equally divided.

(5) The Senate shall choose their other officers and also a President pro tempore, in the absence of the Vice-President, or when he shall exercise the office of President of the United States.

(6) The Senate shall have the sole power to try all impeachments. When sitting for that purpose, they shall be on oath or affirmation. When the President of the United States is tried, the Chief Justice shall preside: and no person shall be convicted without the concurrence of two thirds of the members present.

(7) Judgment in cases of impeachment shall not extend further than to removal from office, and disqualification to hold and enjoy any office of honor, trust or profit under the United States: but the party convicted shall nevertheless be liable and subject to indictment, trial, judgment and punishment, according to law.

ORGANIZATION OF CONGRESS

Section 4. (1) The times, places and manner of holding elections for Senators and Representatives, shall be prescribed in each State by the Legislature thereof; but the Congress may at any time by law make or alter such regulations, (except as to the places of choosing Senators).

(2) The Congress shall assemble at least once in every year, (and such meeting shall be on the first Monday in December,) unless they shall by law appoint a different day.

Section 5. (1) Each House shall be the judge of the elections, returns and qualifications of its own members, and a majority of each shall constitute a quorum to do business; but a smaller number may adjourn day to day, and may be authorized to compel the attendance of absent members, in such manner, and under such penalties as each House may provide.

(2) Each House may determine the rules of its proceedings, punish its members for disorderly behavior, and, with the concurrence of two thirds, expel a member.

(3) Each House shall keep a journal of its proceedings, and from time to time publish the same, excepting such parts as may in their judgment require secrecy; and the yeas and nays of the members of either House on any question shall, at the desire of one fifth of those present, be entered on the journal.

(4) Neither House, during the session of Congress, shall, without the consent of the other, adjourn for more than three days, nor to any other place than that in which the two Houses shall be sitting.

Section 6. (1) The Senators and Representatives shall receive a compensation for their services, to be ascertained by law, and paid out of the Treasury of the United States. They shall in all cases, except treason, felony and breach of the peace, be privileged from arrest during their attendance at the session of their respective Houses, and in going to and returning from the same, and for any speech or debate in either House, they shall not be questioned in any other place.

(2) No Senator or Representative shall, during the time for which he was elected, be appointed to any civil office under the authority of the United States, which shall have been created, or the emoluments whereof shall have been increased during such time; and no person holding any office under the United States, shall be a member of either House during his continuance in office.

Section 7. (1) All bills for raising revenue shall originate in the House of Representatives; but the Senate may propose or concur with amendments as on other bills.

(2) Every bill which shall have passed the House of Representatives and the Senate, shall, before it becomes a law, be presented to the President of the United States; if he approve he shall sign it, but if not he shall return it, with his objections to that House in which it shall have originated, who shall enter the objections at large on their journal, and proceed to reconsider it. If after such reconsideration two thirds of that House shall agree to pass the bill, it shall be sent, together with the objections, to the other House, by which it shall likewise be reconsidered, and if approved by two thirds of that House, it shall become a law. But in all such cases the votes of both Houses shall be determined by yeas and nays, and the names of the persons voting for and against the bill shall be entered on the journal of each House respectively. If any bill shall not be returned by the

APPENDIX 3   217

President within ten days (Sundays excepted) after it shall have been presented to him, the same shall be a law, in like manner as if he had signed it, unless the Congress by their adjournment prevent its return, in which case it shall not be a law.

(3) Every order, resolution, or vote to which the concurrence of the Senate and House of Representatives may be necessary (except on a question of adjournment) shall be presented to the President of the United States; and before the same shall take effect, shall be approved by him, or being disapproved by him, shall be repassed by two thirds of the Senate and House of Representatives, according to the rules and limitations prescribed in the case of a bill.

POWERS VESTED IN CONGRESS

Section 8. The Congress shall have power:

(1) To lay and collect taxes, duties, imposts and excises, to pay the debts and provide for the common defense and general welfare of the United States; but all duties, imposts and excises shall be uniform throughout the United States;

(2) To borrow money on the credit of the United States;

(3) To regulate commerce with foreign nations, and among the several States, and with the Indian tribes;

(4) To establish an uniform rule of naturalization, and uniform laws on the subject of bankruptcies throughout the United States;

(5) To coin money, regulate the value thereof, and of foreign coin, and fix the standard of weights and measures;

(6) To provide for the punishment of counterfeiting the securities and current coin of the United States;

(7) To establish post offices and post roads;

(8) To promote the progress of science and useful arts, by securing for limited times to authors and inventors the exclusive right to their respective writings and discoveries;

(9) To constitute tribunals inferior to the Supreme Court;

(10) To define and punish piracies and felonies committed on the high seas, and offenses against the law of nations;

(11) To declare war, grant letters of marque and reprisal, and make rules concerning captures on land and water;

(12) To raise and support armies, but no appropriation of money to that use shall be for a longer term than two years;

(13) To provide and maintain a navy;

(14) To make rules for the government and regulation of the land and naval forces;

(15) To provide for calling forth the militia to execute the laws of the Union, suppress insurrections and repel invasions;

(16) To provide for organizing, arming, and disciplining, the militia, and for governing such part of them as may be employed in the service of the United States, reserving to the States respectively, the appointment of the officers, and the authority of training the militia according to the discipline prescribed by Congress;

(17) To exercise exclusive legislation in all cases whatsoever, over such district (not exceeding ten miles square) as may, by cession of particular States, and the acceptance of Congress, become the seat of the Government of the United States, and to exercise like authority over all places purchased by the consent of the legislature of the State in which the same shall be for the erection of forts, magazines, arsenals, dockyards, and other needful buildings; and

(18) To make all laws which shall be necessary and proper for carrying into execution the foregoing powers, and all other powers vested by this Constitution in the Government of the United States, or in any department or office thereof.

RESTRAINTS, FEDERAL AND STATE

Section 9. (1) The migration or importation of such persons as any of the States now existing shall think proper to admit, shall not be prohibited by the Congress prior to the year one thousand eight hundred and eight, but a tax or duty may be imposed on such importation, not exceeding ten dollars for each person.

(2) The privilege of the writ of habeas corpus shall not be suspended, unless when in cases of rebellion or invasion the public safety may require it.

(3) No bill of attainder or ex post facto law shall be passed.

(4) No capitation, (or other direct,) tax shall be laid unless in proportion to the census or enumeration herein before directed to be taken.

(5) No tax or duty shall be laid on articles exported from any State.

(6) No preference shall be given by any regulation of commerce or revenue to the parts of one State over those of another: nor shall vessels bound to, or from, one State, be obliged to enter, clear, or pay duties in another.

(7) No money shall be drawn from the Treasury, but in consequence of appropriations made by law; and a regular statement and account of the receipts and expenditures of all public money shall be published from time to time.

(8) No title of nobility shall be granted by the United States; and no person holding any office of profit or trust under them, shall, without the consent of the Congress, accept of any present, emolument, office, or title, of any kind whatever, from any king, prince or foreign State.

Section 10. (1) No State shall enter into any treaty, alliance, or confederation, grant letters of marque and reprisal, coin money, emit bills of credit; make anything but gold and silver coin a tender in payment of debts; pass any bill of attainder ex post facto law, or law impairing the obligation of contracts, or grant any title of nobility.

(2) No State shall, without the consent of the Congress, lay any imposts or duties on imports or exports, except what may be absolutely necessary for executing its inspection laws: and the net produce of all duties and imposts, laid by any State on imports or exports, shall be for the use of the Treasury of the United States; and all such laws shall be subject to the revision and control of the Congress.

(3) No State shall, without the consent of Congress, lay any duty of tonnage, keep troops, or ships of war in time of peace, enter into any agreement or compact with another State, or with a foreign power, or engage in war, unless actually invaded, or in such imminent danger as will not admit of delay.

APPENDIX 4

DESIGN FOR WORLD HARMONY
THROUGH LAW AND EXAMPLE

PHASE 1	PHASE 2	PHASE 3	PHASE 4
STUDY LAWS (BACKGROUND)	UNDERSTAND FREEDOM (CONTAINED IN U.S. CONSTITUTION)	INTEGRATE PRINCIPLES AND BELIEFS	EXEMPLIFY THE POWER AND PLEASURE OF PASSIONATE LIVING
10 COMMANDMENTS (MOSAIC LAW)	FREEDOM OF ECONOMIC ENTERPRISE	CONSTANT PERSUIT AND APPLICATION OF TRUTH	CONFIDENCE— (FREEDOM FROM HUMAN FEARS)
SERMON ON THE MOUNT (CHRISTIAN LAW)	FREEDOM OF SPIRITUAL ENTERPRISE	RIGOROUSLY PURSUE AND APPLY TEACHINGS OF CHRIST	SERENITY (FREEDOM FROM DESTRUCTIVE FEARS)
U.S. CONSTITUTION (DEMOCRATIC LAW)	FREEDOM OF SOCIAL ENTERPRISE	MASTER THE TECHNIQUES OF TOTAL POSITIVISM	ABUNDANCE (FREEDOM FROM MATERIAL WANT)
DECLARATION OF INDEPENDENCE (LAW OF HUMAN DIGNITY)	FREEDOM OF POLITICAL ENTERPRISE	INTELLECTUALLY RELATE AND BLEND THESE LAWS AND PRINCIPLES	ACHIEVEMENT (THROUGH USE— NOT FEAR OF LAW)
RESEARCH	PLAN	ORGANIZE	COMMUNICATE

NOTE TO READER: DO YOU HAVE THE COURAGE TO REALLY THINK ABOUT THIS DESIGN?—TO USE IT AS A SET OF STANDARDS AND GOALS FOR THE REST OF YOUR LI-FE?—CAN YOU DARE TO LIVE WITH THE FLAVOR AND THRILL OF TOTAL SUCCESS AS A TOTAL PERSON?

APPENDIX 4

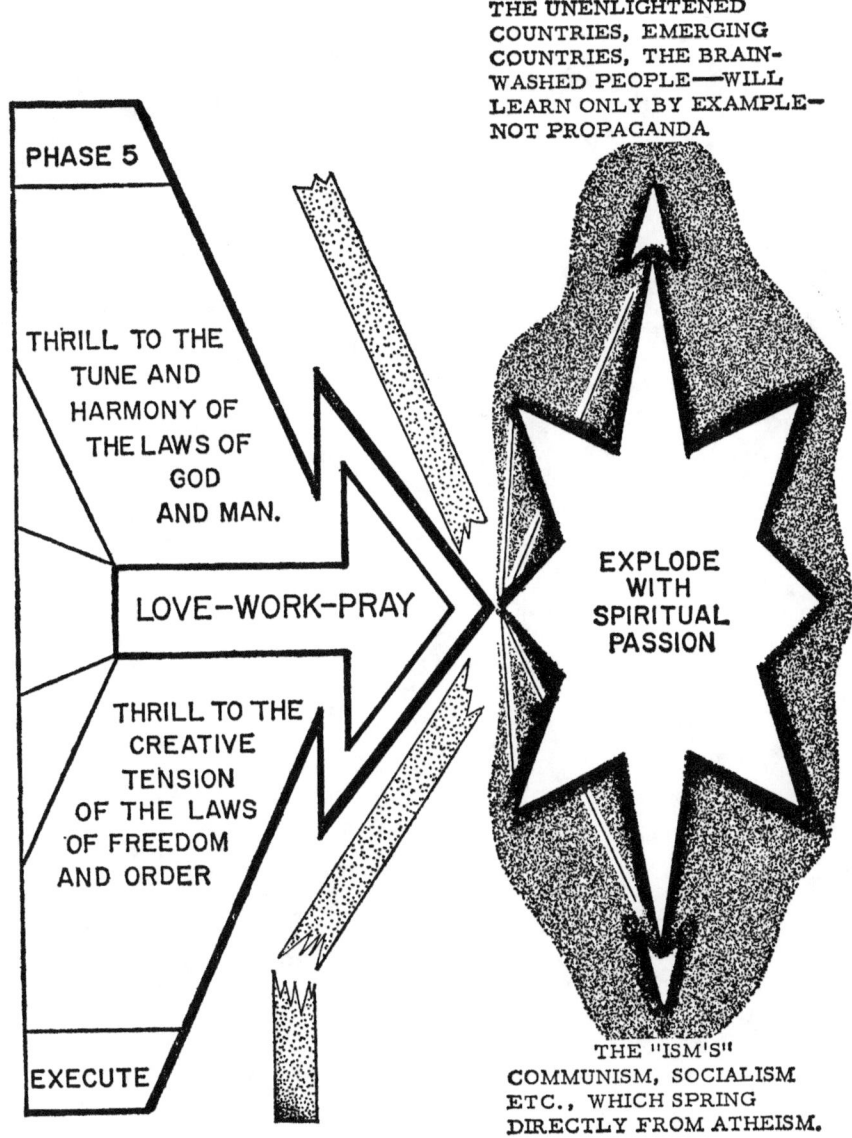

www.ingramcontent.com/pod-product-compliance
Lightning Source LLC
Chambersburg PA
CBHW062027220426
43662CB00010B/1501